A Proposal to Change the Structure of City Planning

Beverly Moss Spatt

The Praeger Special Studies program—utilizing the most modern and efficient book production techniques and a selective worldwide distribution network—makes available to the academic, government, and business communities significant, timely research in U.S. and international economic, social, and political development.

A Proposal to Change the Structure of City Planning

Case Study of New York City

PRAEGER SPECIAL STUDIES IN U.S. ECONOMIC AND SOCIAL DEVELOPMENT

Praeger Publishers   New York   Washington   London

PRAEGER PUBLISHERS
111 Fourth Avenue, New York, N.Y. 10003, U.S.A.
5, Cromwell Place, London S.W.7, England

Published in the United States of America in 1971
by Praeger Publishers, Inc.

© 1971 by Praeger Publishers, Inc.

Library of Congress Catalog Card Number: 72-151958

Printed in the United States of America

TO JOHN M. LEAVENS

If the Administration believes that New
York deserves the benefits of logical
development at a time of critical change
and expansion, one of its first tasks is
a research job. A systematic analysis of
the legal, administrative and political
background of the Commission's peculiar
impotence . . . would clarify the reasons
for the tragi-comedy of planning errors.*

The planning function in the City of New York
is in disarray. Three factors contribute to the
condition: (1) both professional and general understanding of the nature and scope of planning has
broadened substantially over the past five years;
(2) the structure or system for planning in the New
York City government does not especially accommodate
this new understanding; and (3) the style of leadership in recent years has made both professionalism
and meaningful citizen participation difficult.

It is the purpose of this study to examine the
structures for planning, especially the Planning
Commission and the Planning Department, to make
observations on past and current performance, to
suggest the options presently available for new
structures and operational style, and out of these
to suggest what seems to the author to be the most
viable choice.

This volume is in no way meant to be accusative.
The author is aware of her reputation as a critic.
As a Commissioner she has been deeply involved in
issues confronting the Planning Commission and often

---

*"New York Program: Planning," editorial, The
New York Times, December 26, 1965.

has been a minority of one in dissent to actions taken. Clearly this raises the hazard of subjectivity in writing. The author has striven for as high a degree as possible of objectivity and detachment. Hopefully, this study will be viewed as a constructive proposition. Already a few of the author's recommendations are being considered, as evidenced by recent proposals.

September, 1970

SPECIAL ACKNOWLEDGMENT

Perry L. Norton was of invaluable assistance. Without him, this study would not have been written. His development of my proposal, his analytical insight, his encouragement at critical moments, and his warmth and friendship made this book possible.

ACKNOWLEDGMENTS

My deep appreciation to Edwin Friedman, Millard Humstone, and Fred Rosenberg who in varying degrees contributed significantly to my education as a planner and to my effectiveness as a Commissioner.

My thanks to Paul Davidoff, Peter Detmold, Neil Gold, Herman Hellman, and George Raymond for helping me reach this point in time.

My appreciation to former Mayor Robert F. Wagner for appointing me to the New York City Planning Commission and affording me the opportunity of making a contribution to the City of New York.

To my husband Sam and my three children, Robin, Jonathan, and David, my love and thanks for their great patience while I was writing this book and at all times.

CONTENTS

LIST OF FIGURES

Planning is concerned with the unified economic, social, and physical development of a geographic area.* Planning is the "systematic, continuous, forward-looking application of the best intelligence available to programs of common affairs in the public field."** Planning is concerned with the needs of people--recognition, articulation, and resolution of their problems, formation of long-range goals and objectives, systematic analysis of alternative courses of action and their consequences. Planning involves a process: data-gathering, analysis, forecasting, quantitative and qualitative input, constraints, value judgments, assumptions, priorities, testing, evaluation, and reevaluation. Planning is reflective and comprehensive.

Ultimately, the planning decisions regarding the development of our communities are made by the elected representatives of the people. But these decisions may be wasteful of human life and monetary and physical resources unless they are based on:

1. an adequate airing of the issues involved in the many complex policy decisions to be made;

2. an objective view of the facts and values involved in these situations;

---

*Article II of the Constitution of the American Institute of Planners, as amended 1967. See American Institute of Planners, "Report of the Committee on Restatement of Institute Purposes," AIP Newsletter (Washington, D.C.: September, 1965), pp.8-11.

**National Resources Board, "Report" (Washington, D.C.: Library of Congress, 1934).

3. a presentation and comparison of the costs and implications of alternative ways of reaching goals and solving problems; and

4. an analysis of the precise relation of policy-making and specific development decisions to each other and to the economic, social, and physical future of the city.

The task of giving full and comprehensive dimension to the problems, constructing realistic alternatives, coordinating development decisions, and evaluating action in the light of community goals is the task of planning. Planning enlarges the awareness of our elected representatives and the public as to the implications of policy-making and political agreement. These allotted tasks and the goal of a better city cannot be achieved without the steady day-to-day efforts of trained personnel who possess the capacity to deal with the myriad of decisions that the city government must make and who can put the issues into proper perspective for the city's decision-makers.

Patrick Cusick has written that planners have been the scapegoat of society. Although society cries out for planning, it rejects planning as antithetical to the so-called traditional spirit of individualism.* So in casting about for a whipping boy, the cities point to planning as the reason for current inadequacies. Henry Fagin has stated that in reality what should emerge from the cities' frustration in their attempts to "grasp the dynamic urban scene" is a "sense of urgency about the need to improve our planning processes precisely so as to gain the capability of handling the urban complexity, size and interaction."**

---

*Patrick J. Cusick, "The Planner in Emerging Urban Society, A Confrontation," in Proceedings of 1965 Annual Conference of the American Institute of Planners, p. 67.

**Henry Fagin, "Planning for Future Urban Growth," 30 Law and Contemporary Problems 9(1965).

THE PLANNING FUNCTION

1

THE LOCATION OF
PLANNING IN GOVERNMENT:
A REVIEW

A HISTORY OF THE PLANNING MOVEMENT

At the 1915 National Planning Conference, Robert Whitten stated:

> In American state and city government almost every expansion of governmental activity is initiated through the instrumentality of a new Commission. There is a fear of entrusting the working out of a new function to existing officials. Existing officials are already loaded with work and it is thought that they will have neither the time, the inclination nor perhaps the ability to develop the new idea. A new Commission, composed usually of unpaid members, is used to plant and care for the new undertaking, at least during its development period. Often the new function fails to take root as a permanent institution and the Commission dies. If on the other hand, the new function becomes a recognized governmental function, it is sooner or later merged with the general governmental organization. The new function is transferred to the appropriate official department and the Commission disappears.

> The City Planning movement will
> doubtless be no exception to the rule.
> . . . The City plan is so vitally con-
> nected with every phase of municipal
> activity that it must be worked in as
> close touch as is possible with the exist-
> ing administrative and legislative author-
> ities.[1]

The prophetic words of Robert Whitten describe the
history of the planning movement.

Planning generally in the United States has
passed through three stages. During the first stage,
planning was a function of private civic organizations such as the Civic Improvement Committee of the
Chicago Commercial Club. Their basic interest was
in preparing a specific plan for improving the slums,
planning the street system, and creating the "City
Beautiful," not in creating a planning agency.

The second stage was the creation of the independent planning commission, a part of government
in terms of financing, prestige, and implementation
but separate in terms of administrative and legislative
autonomy.

The independent planning commission was proposed
by a 1928 report of the Advisory Committee on City
Planning and Zoning, United States Department of
Commerce. (Three of the nine members of this committee
were Edward M. Bassett, Alfred Bettman, and Frederick
Law Olmstead, Jr., individuals who figure most promi-
nently in the history of United States planning.)
The Committee recommended "A Standard City Planning
Enabling Act" that created a "semi-autonomous" planning commission made up of "objective, non-partisan"
members with "six-year over-lapping terms." This
planning commission was to be "above politics," to
have "technical expertise," and to have legislative
power that could be overridden only by a three-fourths
vote of the municipal legislative body.[2] In those
days, there was a general mistrust of municipal government and the advisory committee believed that it
could sell the enabling act to the state legislatures

only if the planning function were separate from
municipal government, serving as a buffer between
people and government.

According to Hans Spiegal and Stephan Mittenthal,
"The early planning movement was based on a doctrine
which said that what planners needed was great formal
powers, independent of the political process, which
would enable them to act as an autonomous 'fourth
power' in city government."[3] However, this very
independence apparently prevented the planning commission from fulfilling its planning role. Moynihan
suggests that independence leads to isolation and,
eventually, to powerlessness.[4]

The belief that the planning commission should
be semi-autonomous, that it should be above politics,
that the commissioners should have special technical
expertise, and that the commission should serve as
a buffer between government and the people persisted
for many years. In a detailed study, Robert A.
Walker skillfully destroyed these four myths about
an independent planning body.[5]

1. Semi-autonomous.* The difficult three-fourths
veto to override the planning commission thwarts the
legally elected legislative body. The independence
from the administrative branch causes confusion and
conflict. Nonaccountability to the executive office
prevents plans from being implemented.

2. Above Politics. The members of the commission are appointed by the Mayor, a political creature.
The members represent special interests and pressure
groups. Members are usually of upper income and
not representative of the general public; certainly
they are not representative of the low-income groups.
Few appointees have a social welfare view. Most
members have a fear of public criticism and subsequent loss of prestige. As a result, few recommendations are made on controversial issues. The
members function with their past orientation and
prejudices and it is highly questionable whether
they are more objective than elected officials.
        *An attempt follows to synthesize Robert A.
Walker's The Planning Function in Urban Government,
at the risk of doing violence to his arguments.

3. Special Competence--Expertise. The members
are part-time and cannot or do not give enough time
to acquire an understanding of planning. At the
1936 public hearings concerning the creation of a
New York City Planning Commission, Lawrence Orton
stated that "problems are so vast in New York City
that no matter how public spirited the citizens are
it is almost impossible to acquaint themselves with
the essential facts while only giving such time as
they can spare from their profession or business
duties."[6] Most of the planning work is done by the
Chairman and staff and the Commissioners are unable
to become sufficiently educated by only attending
meetings. The average Commissioner has no special
competence or peculiar attitudes enabling him to
exercise a superior judgment.

4. Commission as Interpreter. The commission
is supposed to be a buffer between the technician
and the public but there is little if any interrelationship between the staff and commission members
and between the planning commission and the public.
Few long-range plans have ever been prepared to
interpret to the public. The commission's role as
a buffer between the public and government only
results in confusion within the channels of communication. A citizen advisory committee could serve
the function of interpreter.

Mr. Walker concluded that the independent commission guided planning through its infancy and
that it was time for change in order to deal with
the complexities of modern society. He complimented
the independent planning commission, buried it with
a eulogy, and set the stage for the next phase of
planning--the placing of planning within the governmental structure, a professional function in the
executive office.

Donald H. Webster reinforces Robert Walker's
views concerning the elimination of the independent
planning commission. The chief executive is responsible for policy decisions and if planning is to be
the basis for these decisions, the process must be
an integral part of the executive office and not
kept at arm's length.[7]

The third stage in planning in the United States was related in time to a substantial movement concerned with professionalized management of city functions. The focus of the movement was a federation of agencies located in Chicago--associations for city managers, tax officials, and various state government employees. One of these associations was (and still is) the American Society of Planning Officials. Founded in 1935, its first Executive Director, Walter Blucher, spent twenty solid years promoting and supporting the location of planning in a staff agency in the office of the chief executive.

The movement for professionalized management of city functions was a powerful movement and had many adherents. But it did not lay to rest for all time the concern for the relationship of planning to the local government. Writing on the subject continues into the present time.

THE CURRENT DISCUSSION

T. J. Kent, Jr., believes that the independent planning commission is neither responsible to the government nor to the people and that its independence is contrary to democratic procedures. The location of the planning function must be considered in terms of the primary client as well as the basic political realities. According to Mr. Kent, the City Council is not only the primary client but also the imple-mentor of planning decisions. If legislative decisions are to reflect the plan, the decision-makers must participate in plan-making. Mr. Kent recognizes the duality of planning and the need for planning to relate to the executive as well as to the legislative branch of government.[8]

Robert Walker and T. J. Kent, Jr., both recognize the fact that planning is political as well as pro-fessional and technical in nature. They both clearly indicate the choices: the independent planning com-mission, planning located in the office of the chief executive, or planning as a policy-making activity of the legislative body.

In a recent study, Edward Logue recommends that the planning function in New York City be placed within the executive office, subsumed under the Housing and Development Administration:

> With so little evidence of city planning
> it is no wonder that there is such a star-
> tling variety of notions about city
> planning and what is its proper place in
> the scheme of things. . . . city planning
> [should] be taken out of its present
> ambivalent position of Delphic Oracle,
> Court of Last Resort, Spot Planner and
> Decision Maker on routine map and zoning
> changes, and placed with the related
> functions principally concerned with
> making plans happen.[9]

He writes that no one in New York maintains that the New York City Planning Commission has done a proper job of city planning; that the proponents of city planning, as defined by an independent commission, all embracing, are defending ineffective planning. In answer to the argument that an independent planning commission is needed to give the citizenry an objective and nonpartisan hearing on controversial measures, Mr. Logue states that "we have not been overwhelmed with the number of occasions when the City Planning Commission has asserted its independence and gone against the wishes of the Mayor in office."[10] He agrees with Robert Walker and T. J. Kent, Jr., that a nonpaid planning advisory council would be suffi-cient.

The forthright recommendations of Edward Logue came at a time when civic groups were not yet ready to accept the elimination of the independent planning commission. In addition, most civic groups did not believe that planning was just an element of action, merely for purposes of urban renewal. Robert B. Mitchell opposed the placing of planning in a devel-opment agency, although he admitted that there was a need for a new form for a central planning unit, perhaps a planning-budgeting staff.[11]

Community Service Society, while recognizing
that the "planning machinery could be improved,"
wrote that "no one city administrative agency should
or can act as a general planning body."[12] Citizens'
Housing and Planning Council summed up the general
feeling in its statement "that the public--at least
the editorial writers--will not easily consent to
the amputation of this independent Tribunal."[13]

The question is, who is the primary client of
planning. If the planning commission is maintained
as an independent agency, the plan may be advisory,
adopted and embraced only by the commission. If
planning is placed in the executive office, the
chief executive may not be interested in long-range
plans and comprehensive goals. If the legislative
body is the client, the legislative body may base
its legislative decision on a plan that it has helped
to make, but the executive branch is the initiator
of policy for which plans should be the basis.

Richard Bolan questions how to make planning
more effective and more acceptable and how to create
an agency that will respond to the values within the
city and at the same time influence community social
choices. He submits that it is necessary to consider
the decision-making environment and the dynamics of
decision-making and to adapt the planning process
to the new complexities.[14]

More and more writers in the planning field
reiterate this idea. Robinson Everett and Richard
Leach write that planning "is irrevocably linked
with politics, and what appears at first blush to be
merely a technical problem becomes finally a complex
political problem."[15] David Craig writes that "no
planning program will be effective unless it is led
by the Mayor."[16] William Rafsky believes that there
must be a close relationship between planners and
the elected officials so that "the planners develop
the alternative strategies and provide the best
possible guidelines for policy formulation to the
elected decision-maker."[17] Harvey Perloff states
that the purpose and effectiveness of planning depend
on the manner in which planning is organized within

government. He submits that the future focus and
location of the planning staff will be in the executi-
office.[18] Frederick Gutheim writes that the planners
now must be aware of practical politics and have an
understanding of politicians and political decision-
making.[19] Charles Ascher writes that "in more and
more cities where there is a responsible chief executive officer, the planner is attached to him. The
independent city planning commission is a relic of
the 1920's."[20]

Henry Fagin offers an important contribution to
the planning dialogue with specific, detailed recommendations as to the future process and location of
planning.[21] He unequivocally states that the independent city planning commission, as a deliberating
body, a supervisory body, a coordinating body, and a
body acting as a buffer between the people and government, should be eliminated. These functions
should be the responsibility of elected officials.
The independent commission limits understanding of
the proper position of planning in government and
prevents proper recognition by the chief executive.
Mr. Fagin agrees with Walker, Kent, and Logue that
the independent role can be played by a citizen
group and that such a group will offer better objective advice and criticism than a hand-picked lay
commission. Mr. Fagin rejects the legislature as
the client of planning, contending that the legislatur
is not the ultimate decision-making branch. In his
opinion, the executive is the creator of policy and
the coordinator of activities. The scope of planning
is as broad as government and planning must be the
basis for all governmental activities.

Mr. Fagin recommends a professional planning
agency within the executive branch headed by an
appointed planning officer responsible to the chief
executive. This "Central Planning Agency" would be
responsible for total plan formulation and for modification and coordination of department plans. The
central agency would be comprehensive, a synthesis
of different areas of disciplines--mathematical,
architectural, economic, geographic, political, and
sociological. It would be concerned with all matters--

physical, social, economic, and fiscal. Each department would have its own planning section which would
work within its functional areas but within an overall
city framework established by the central agency.
Henry Fagin believes that with "disciplined research,
creative invention, and activity coordination,"[22]
the purpose of planning will be achieved. He concludes
that only with professional planning structured in
the executive office will the city be able to make
intelligent, coherent decisions.

Some of the literature in the late 1960's discusses planning as a part of the planning-programming-
budgeting system. However, Yehezkel Dror writes
that planning is a political process and not just a
resource allocation. In his view, planning blends
quantitative methodology with qualitative methodology
and political knowledge and understanding. He foresees
for the planner a new professional role within the
executive branch of government, as a policy analyst
who is a member of a kitchen cabinet, advisory to
the top decision-maker.[23]

Richard Bolan has expertise and experience in
quantitative systems. Although he admits the importance of mathematical models and computer systems
that can analyze millions of facts, he submits that
the best method is that which offers choices for the
future and requires value judgments:

> Today's effective planner is not found
> behind a computer console. Mathematical
> models and games have utility in planning
> but theirs is a sharply limited utility.
> Creativity, imagination and innovation do
> not lurk in their parameters. Man and his
> mind are still the only important agents
> of planning. And, intrinsically involved
> is a collaboration of many men and many
> minds interacting in social and cultural
> settings, making value judgments about
> their preferred future.[24]

NOTES

1. Quoted by Perry L. Norton in "Introductory Notes to Some History and Concepts on Urban Planning," (New York: New York University, 1970), p. 31 (class notes, not available for purchase).

2. United States Dept. of Commerce, "Report of the Advisory Committee on City Planning and Zoning, 1928.

3. Hans B. C. Spiegal, and Stephan D. Mittenthal Neighborhood Power and Control: Implications for Urban Planning, (New York: Institute of Urban Environment, Columbia University School of Architecture, 1968), p. 62. The classification of planning as the "fourth power" is attributed to Rexford Tugwell, first Chairman of the New York City Planning Commission.

4. Daniel P. Moynihan, Maximum Feasible Misunderstanding: Community Action in the War on Poverty, (New York: The Free Press, 1969).

5. Robert A. Walker, The Planning Function in Urban Government (Chicago: University of Chicago Press, 1950).

6. Ibid.

7. Donald H. Webster, Urban Planning and Municipal Public Policy, (New York: Harper Brothers, 1955).

8. T. J. Kent, Jr., The Urban General Plan (San Francisco: Chandler Publishing Co., 1964).

9. Edward J. Logue, Chairman, Let There Be Commitment, Report of a Study Group of the Institute of Public Administration to Mayor John V. Lindsay, (New York: Institute of Public Administration, September, 1966), p. V (italics mine).

10.   Ibid, p. 2.

11.   Robert B. Mitchell, Consultant to the New York City Dept. of City Planning, in an unpublished letter to Edward J. Logue (New York: Planning Commission Files, October 3, 1966).

12.   Community Service Society, "Letter to Mr. Edward J. Logue" (New York, August 31, 1966).

13.   Citizens' Housing and Planning Council, Housing and Planning News, XXIV, 8-9, (July-August, 1966), 5.

14.   Richard S. Bolan, "Emerging Views of Planning" Journal of the American Institute of Planners, (July, 1967), 233-45.

15.   Robinson O. Everett and Richard H. Leach, "Urban Problems and Prospects" Law and Contemporary Problems, XXX, (Winter, 1965), 2.

16.   David W. Craig, "The Personnel Criterion in the Planning Program," in American Society of Planning Officials, Planning 1969 (Chicago, 1969), p. 53.

17.   William A. Rafsky, "Checkpoints for Evaluating the Planning Program," in American Society of Planning Officials, op. cit., p. 79.   .

18.   Harvey Perloff, ed., Planning and the Urban Community (Pittsburgh: University of Pittsburgh Press, 1961), "Introduction."

19.   Frederick Gutheim, "The Politics of the Metropolis," in Perloff, ed., op. cit.

20.   Charles S. Ascher in an unpublished letter to Citizens' Housing and Planning Council, (undated).

21.   Henry Fagin, "Planning Organization and Activities Within the Framework of Urban Government," in Perloff, ed., op. cit.

22.   Ibid.

23.   Yehezkel Dror, "Policy Analysts: A New
Professional Role in Government Service," Public
Administration Review, (September, 1967), 197-203.

24.   Richard S. Bolan, "New Rules for Judging
Analytical Techniques in Urban Planning," paper
presented at the 1970 National Planning Conference,
American Society of Planning Officials, April, 1970.

Against the background of the preceding general
history we will now examine the situation in New
York City.*

"The placement of the planning function in the
decision-making system is determined largely by
forces outside of the planning field."[1] So it was
that the authors of the 1938 New York City Charter,
in response to a general mistrust of municipal politics, established an independent planning commission
free from executive control:

> The Commission was made up of members who
> were committed to the premise that the
> commission should be an institution of
> experts with an authoritative voice in
> the decisions of city government, yet be

_____

*The conclusions noted in Chapters 2-7 are the
results of an empirical study of three years' duration.
Interviews were conducted with about 40 members of
the Planning Department staff (some of whom are no
longer with the agency) and with officials and staff
of other City agencies. Systematic analysis of the
function and performance of the Planning Commission
and Planning Department forms the basis for these
sections of the study.

itself aloof and protected, without the
necessity of bargaining with and making
concessions to the politicians and special
interests.2

Over the years, it seems that its very independence has prevented the Planning Commission from
fulfilling its proper role. Mayors have been unwilling
to embrace plans made by people not responsive or
responsible to them and, as a result, a certain iner-
tia on the part of the City Planning Commission
appeared. A Master Plan was never developed, initi-
ative was lost, and public relations were damaged.
Those plans that may have been made were not supported
by the political branches of government and, thus,
the plans were ineffectual for lack of implementation.

Since 1938, the involvement of municipal government has spread into all areas of development and
service. Local community participation has assumed
new proportions. Yet planning, which should be the
basis for the many complex decisions, has remained
insulated from the decision-making process. With
this fact in mind, in writing the present Charter
(Effective January 1, 1963) the Cahill Charter Revision
Commission provided that the Chairman of the Planning
Commission serve at the pleasure of the Mayor. It
did so with the belief that a closer working relationship between the Mayor and the Commission would make
for more effective planning. In November, 1966,
pursuant to the new charter provisions, Mayor Lindsay
appointed as Chairman his personal aide and Counsel,
Donald H. Elliott.

The Citizens' Housing and Planning Council
suggests that the close relationship between the
Chairman and the Mayor has created problems. Whereas
the Planning Commission now should have been able to
"sway the administration toward the use of the
planning instrument for the design of official policy,"
the Commission has become an instrument of policy,
rather than an initiator. The Mayor has several
times announced that the City would carry out housing
programs (Chelsea Walk was one such) apparently having
forgotten that an independent planning commission

might have blocked the project altogether."3

The Chairman of the Planning Commission's close-
ness to the Mayor also results in conflict and competition with other City departments. Citizens' Housing
and Planning Council comments on the "tug of war"
that has developed between the Planning Commission
and the Housing and Development Administration and
states that the "Planning Commission is favored by
its close links to Mayor Lindsay." Citizens' Housing
and Planning Council further questions whether the
Commission can any longer make independent judgments
and comments that "if the Planning Commission cannot
maintain real independence, one must wonder how to
justify institutional independence."4

The tenure and overlapping terms of Planning
Commission members were meant to provide safeguards
against political intervention and control by a
single Mayor. Today, independence is rarely seen
on the Commission. At one point, at the end of
Mayor Lindsay's first term, a vocal minority of three
(against the majority of four) developed on an important issue. This minority, consisting of Commissioners
Harmon Goldstone, Elinor Guggenheimer, and Beverly
Moss Spatt, was short-lived: the Mayor soon appointed
Mr. Goldstone to chair the Landmarks Preservation
Commission and did not reappoint Mrs. Guggenheimer,
whose term had expired. In the meantime, Commissioner
James Sweeney, a holdover from the previous administration, died. As a result, the Chairman of the Planning
Commission and five of its six members were appointees
of Mayor Lindsay. Mrs. Spatt's term was completed
and she was not reappointed. All members are appointees of the present Mayor.

One Planning Commission member is assistant to
the head of the Liberal Party. In appointing another
member, the Mayor stated that this member would
represent Queens and speak for that Borough on the
Planning Commission. This was so contrary to the
past independence of the Commission that the then
Vice-Chairman of the Commission, Lawrence Orton, felt
compelled to issue a "Memorandum to Chairman Elliott.
(September 11, 1969) rejecting the Mayor's statement.

He wrote, "as you know, my greatest concern over the
years has been the evolution of the City Planning
Commission and Department as an institution of goverr
ment. A basic principle ever since our organization
began has been that members do not represent particul
constituencies." He went on to say that such a
practice is "frowned on in principle" and in the
past was "kept to a bare minimum in practice."5

     Several analyses of the Commission conclude
that the Commission members rarely dissent for fear
of loss of prestige. This is apparently the case.
Several Commissioners expressed extreme dissatisfacti
with the proposed Master Plan, yet only one publicly
dissented. Shortly after, this dissenting Commission
and another Commissioner wrote a joint dissent on
another issue (West Village Housing), but fear of
association caused the latter Commissioner to disasso
ciate himself. When there is disagreement among the
Commission members, great pressures are exerted.
The vote on the United Nations Development Corporatio
Plan was laid over many times because of opposition
to the Plan by five of the Commissioners. Political
pressures were brought to bear. Finally, a formal
vote was taken; there were four in favor and three
opposed. Two of those in favor wrote reports stating
that they were still opposed to the Plan but had been
persuaded to vote for it. The Mayor had publicly
committed himself and the City to this Plan. The
Chairman of the Planning Commission was also a member
of the United Nations Development Corporation.

     The present Mayor does not view the Commission
as independent of the executive office. At a meeting
between the Mayor and the author (summer, 1969), he
stated that he views the Commission as his agency.
The job of the Chairman is "to ride herd on the
departments" carrying out his policies. The Commissioners are to go along with the Chairman or else
"want out."

     Under the Lindsay administration, the New York
City Planning Commission has evolved into a dual
agency. On one hand, there is the independent Planning Commission made up of the Chairman, who serves

at the pleasure of the Mayor, and six members with
tenure who presumably are not responsible to the
Mayor. The members are separated from the professional staff, acting without their expertise. On
the other hand, the Chairman (according to the City
Charter) is also Director of the City Planning
Department and, as such, supervises the professional
work.

Given this dual arrangement, the Chairman had
an option: by virtue of his chairmanship, he could
convene and utilize the Commission as an important
deliberative body or he could choose to treat the
Commission as a defunct appendage and call for its
involvement only when the statutes so required. He
opted for this second choice. The self-isolation of
the Chairman from the Commissioners is virtually
complete.

The Commission meets only every Monday after-
noon for an executive session, every other Wednesday
for a public hearing, and at occasional special
sessions. Attendance is poor and a quorum may be
lacking. Commission site inspections are rare and
the Commission has no understanding of the sites in
terms of the actual visible community, the services,
the amenities of the circulation patterns, the physical, social, and economic conditions. There are
many items on Monday's executive agenda, but presentations and discussions are superficial. Recommendations
are brought before the Commission with very little
background material and seldom with any delineation
of alternative possibilities. The uncertainty absorp-
tion factor is very apparent and information is watered
down and redirected before being submitted to the
Commission. Important decisions which, by statute,
require the Commission's approval often are brought
to the Commission at a date too late to allow for
serious consideration. Approval is requested, is
forthcoming, but is uninformed.

This style of operation naturally obviates a
qualitative involvement of the Commission. It has
induced a special phenomenon known as the "super
executive session," which follows the Commission's

Monday meeting and is attended only by the Chairman, the Commission members, and a few selected top staff members. At these sessions, the Chairman is able to dictate the outcome of most of the items because of the Commission's lack of familiarity with the subject matter. On more controversial, well-publicized issues, the vote is often deferred until a politicall acceptable decision is reached.

Given the choice made by the Chairman on the Commission's operation, one might then assume that the staff of the Planning Department (of which the Chairman serves as Director) has become strong and effective as a counterbalance to the weakness and ineffectiveness of the Commission. This is not the case.

NOTES

1. Henry Cohen, "The Changing Role of the Planner in the Decision-Making Process," in Ernest Erber, ed., Urban Planning in Transition, (New York: Grossman Press, 1970), p. 174.

2. Philip Selznick, TVA and the Grass Roots: A Study in the Sociology of Formal Organization (New York: Harper Torchbooks, 1966) p. 220.

3. Citizens' Housing and Planning Council, Housing and Planning News XXVI, 4-5 (January-February 1968), 5. (The Planning Commission did block the Chelsea Walk Project after a severe conflict involving the Chairman, the Commission, the planning staff, and the Mayor.)

4. Ibid.

5. Lawrence Orton, "Memorandum to Chairman Elliott," Sept. 11, 1969 (Files of City Planning Commission).

3

THE PLANNING
DEPARTMENT STAFF

The dubious clubhouse mystique of conven-
tional political wisdom is no substitute
for the necessary tools of modern management. What is required is the best that
technology and philosophy can contribute
toward the survival of the cities.[1]

The dual role of the planning agency and the
separation (informal) of the Planning Department
from the Commission has neither enhanced the
Department's administrative role nor its professionalism. Professionalism and administration within an
agency must be considered together; the two facets
are interrelated and mutually supportive. How the
administrators relate to the professionals and how
the planners are used and their efficiency maximized
are administrative problems as well as professional
problems. Without competent professionals there is
no product, but without competent administrators
the product is minimal. The role of the professional
planner is to research, analyze, advise, and inform.
In the case of the New York City Planning Department,
the personal dominance exerted by the Chairman over
the staff limits its role to the area of "housekeeping
activities."[2] The antiprofessionalism, the lack of
accountability in the Community Renewal Program,
and the frequent use of consultants have resulted
in the demoralization of the staff and the diminution
of professional work.

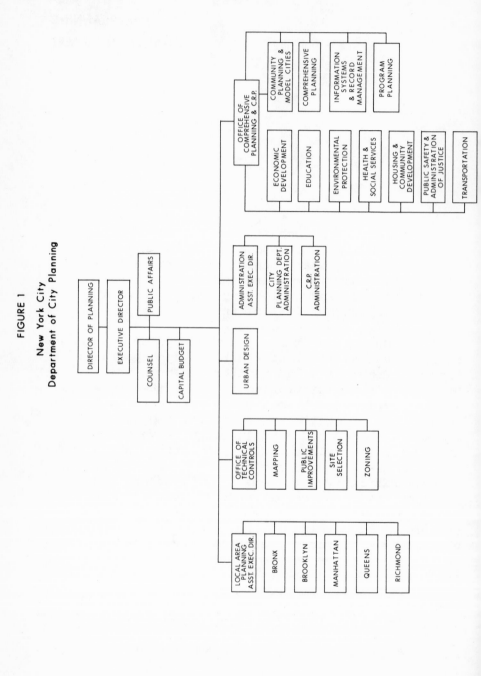

FIGURE 1

New York City
Department of City Planning

THE CURRENT STRUCTURE

The New York City Planning Department staff is made up of about 400 members in three categories: civil service employees, Community Renewal Program staff, and members of the Comprehensive Planning Section. At the head of the Department of City Planning is the Chairman of the Planning Commission who is Director of Planning. On the formal organization chart, the Executive Director is under the Chairman and has the responsibility for coordinating and executing the Department's policies and programs. The Deputy Executive Director of Public Affairs is on the next lower level. Informally, he is on a very high level, with a large staff and a great deal of power.

In 1970, the New York City Department of Personnel notified the Chairman of the Planning Commission that it would not certify the acting Executive Director because he did not meet the minimal qualifications for that position. As a result, the Chairman eliminated the formal position of Executive Director and transferred all its responsibilities to the position of Director of Comprehensive Planning. The acting Executive Director merely assumed a new title. At the same time, the Director of Public Affairs was given the additional title of Director of Administration.

Currently, the Planning Department is run by this triumvirate--Chairman of the Planning Commission, Director of Comprehensive Planning, and Director of Public Affairs. The actual decision-making process is through this group and not through the legally constituted Planning Commission. This arrogation of power to people without the necessary qualifications comes at a time when the Mayor of the City of New York has publicly stated that "the issue is better government" and "professional management experts."

In any analysis of the Planning Department, the reasons underlying the abolition of the position of

Executive Director become relevant. The position of
Executive Director requires expertise and experience
in physical management, in personnel management, in
critical negotiations with federal, state, and local
government and private groups, and most important,
competent understanding of the planning function and
process. The Chairman, in a June 15, 1970, "Memorandum," stated that "The Department of City Planning
has grown enormously both in the scope of its activity
and the size of its staff. . . . Our organizational
structure has to grow with us. Accordingly, I have
decided to abolish the position of Executive Director
and redistribute the responsibilities of the position."[3] It is for the very reasons stated in the
memorandum that the preservation of such a job becomes
even more important. The Chairman's statement indicates a total lack of understanding of the need for
a competent Executive Director to direct, coordinate,
and relate to the large departmental staff. The
elimination of the job of Executive Director reflects
a lack of desire for professional input as a basis
for decision-making as well as a lack of interest in
the proper administration of the agency. It is a
contradiction and a repudiation of modern public
administration practices and techniques.

Prior to the recent reshuffling, the Department
had a Director of Professional Resources (personnel)
and a Director of Administration and Fiscal Management.
These two qualified people were high on the table of
organization but actually had very little control in
their areas. Most of the appointments to the staff,
as well as the administrative decisions, were made
by the acting Executive Director or the Chairman.
The Director of Administration and Fiscal Management
was blocked by the acting Executive Director and had
no prerogative to make decisions pursuant to his
function. The Director of Professional Resources,
whose responsibilities were recruitment, placement,
and training, was unable to establish in-training
programs, bring orderly administrative procedures
into the agency, establish professional recruitment
qualifications, or recruit minority staff members.
(An analysis revealed about a dozen black or Puerto
Rican members of the professional staff.)

STAFF TURNOVER AND LACK OF MOTIVATION

The current almost total demoralization commenced
a few years ago, when an exodus began of highly
trained, experienced, competent staff from high-level
supervisory positions. An actual count indicates
that in December, 1966, there was a staff of 196
professionals and semiprofessionals. Three years
later, 91 of the 196 had left, a turnover of almost
50 percent. Fifty-two staff members hired since
1966 also have left. This exodus occurred even
though staff salaries and fringe benefits have increased. Those with vested (pension) interests also
have left. Not only has the rate of turnover increased
but also the length of time individuals remain in the
Planning Department has critically lessened. It
would seem that the new Chairman was no longer interested in keeping capable planning experts. Not
knowing how or not desiring to use the existing
talent, the Chairman's decisions were gut decisions,
not based on variables and probabilities. Apparently,
the planning administrators did not rely on the staff
to bring them important work and strategic thinking;
therefore, many of the administrators' decisions
resulted in tactical blunders. And so the scene was
set: an agency with no professional substance or
focus; an agency with severe administrative inadequacy;
an agency whose leadership is doing too many things
and not doing anything adequately; an agency that
lacks understanding of and sensitivity to the problems
of the City's residents.

The latent staff demoralization that had existed
for several years became overt in 1969. Impetus was
given by the February 19, 1969 public protest of
five planners from the City Planning Department in
a "Statement of the Rezoning of Parts of Second and
Third Avenue." (Urban Underground, New York, 1969).
Their protest against the Planning Commission was
reinforced by a petition signed by over 100 planners,
including present and former members of the Planning
Department. The five planners stated that: "by
keeping quiet about what they really know ought to
be done, the City Planning Commission has been able

to operate free of any constraints by the public at
large;" that the rezoning of Third Avenue was "counter to policy developed by the department and presented in the staff reports"; that the staff was
"asked to violate their personal integrity by justi-
fying decisions to the public on a technical basis
when they were made on a political level"; and that
"valuable work done by the City Planning Commission
staff and their consultants were kept in inaccessible
files."

The tension within the agency is not limited to
the "Young Turks" but is prevalent throughout the
Planning Department. The Planning Department has
been greatly expanded but hiring is done without any
rationale. There are no work programs, no time
schedules, no attempts to motivate the professional
staff, and no attempts to build up the staff or to
develop information. The staff is indignant when it
sees $100,000 consultant contracts rushed through
while promised salary increases of a couple of
hundred dollars materialize slowly, if ever. The
sum of $10-15,000 is used to construct a model of
Midtown Manhattan (have budget, must spend) while
two planners sit at one desk because, apparently,
staff working conditions are not considered that
important.

The role of the planner within the agency has
been denigrated. For example, the Division of
Operations Planning has been totally decimated.
Among its many responsibilities was the evaluation
of proposed zoning changes. The Division of Operation
Planning established the planning framework in terms
of short, intermediate, and long-term planning considerations as against day-to-day expediency. Plan
determinations are now the exclusive province of the
architects and zoning changes are made according to
what will achieve the best-designed building. In
the Midtown Planning Office, the planners are in the
minority (12 architects, 6 planners--3 of these 6
have left). The architects are not only allocated
two-thirds of the jobs but also get more than their
proportionate share of the total salaries paid to
the professionals. The office is run by an architect

and there can be no doubt that the office has an
aesthetic orientation with the input being primarily
architectural. The majority of the architects on
this staff have neither a past planning background
nor a current interest in long-range goals, interlinkages, and planning processes. This imbalance
has contributed to the planners' low morale. Admit-
tedly, design has been neglected in the past, but
now the pendulum has swung completely over to design
without any consideration of basic planning concepts.
It is a return to the planning approach of the early
1900's, the "City Beautiful" with its images and
monuments.

An example of staff frustration is noted in the
area of transportation. A transportation group was
formed with input from and coordination with the
Metropolitan Transportation Authority, the City Planning Department Manhattan Office, the Midtown and
Lower Manhattan Offices, and the Transportation and
Zoning Sections of the Planning Department. The
group met about twice a week for four to five months
to work on establishing a parking policy. An informal
presentation was made to the Planning Commission but
no Commission policy was established. When the
Chairman and his top staff made parking decisions,
this transportation group was never consulted and
decisions were not professional ones. This group
made numerous attempts to discuss its work with the
Chairman and the acting Executive Director of the
Planning Department, but to no avail. The Chrysler
Structure (41st-42nd Streets, 11th-12th Avenues,
Manhattan) was programmed for about 600 service
stalls and 2,000 spaces for cars without consultation
with the transportation group. The decision was made
without any understanding of the amount of traffic
that would be generated and where the movements
would be. In the long run, such decision-making
is a disadvantage to the public; in the short run,
it is demoralizing to the professionals within the
agency.

The Communications Committee

Agency unrest had increased to a point where, in Spring 1969, the Chairman created a Communications Committee. Several meetings were held with little result. Recommendations were presented by the staff to the acting Executive Director. They have neither been adopted nor presented to the Commission members. Over and above the professional grievances, the Recommendations stated that actions regarding the staff were apparently arbitrary and based on no formal institutionalized procedure for review and evaluation.[4] Communication between management and staff supervisors is poor, and since the supervisory staff has little to say in decision-making, hiring, salaries, and promotions are more often based on personal relationships with the Chairman, the acting Executive Director and the Deputy Executive Director. In an agency as large as the City Planning Department, orderly administrative and management procedures are prerequisites for proper functioning.

Citizens Union's "Statement" at the 1970/71 Executive Budget Public Hearing (June 3, 1970) spoke to the matter of management-employee relationship. Citizens Union stated that the City "is doing very little about employee motivation." It suggested that "one approach is to staff top and middle management positions throughout the government with persons familiar with modern management techniques." It recommended "more efficient use of professionals" and "greater emphasis on in-service training." It gave a "word of caution. This kind of program will not succeed if it is devised by the City unilaterally. It must be a joint management-labor undertaking."[5]

The Community Renewal
Program's Lack of Accountability

A major activity of the City Planning Department is the Community Renewal Program. This program was instituted in New York City in 1961. It is funded two-thirds by the federal government and one-third

by the City.   The program "assesses the City's
overall renewal needs and available resources to
meet them, and spells out the interrelated policies
which comprise the City's current renewal strategy."6
Robert Mitchell, a consultant to the Planning Commission, is head of the Community Renewal Program.
Recently, he expressed great concern about the
turmoil prevalent in this Program.   In May, 1970, at
a Community Renewal Program staff meeting, he stated
that the staff formerly played an integral role in
decision-making.   It was able to gather data, make
value judgments, and come up with proposals that
were not only accepted but desired by the top staff.
Whereas the Planning Department now does not seem to
be involved in resolving any major problems or
formulating any major policies.   Mr. Mitchell also
expressed deep concern about the unusually large
staff turnover in the Community Renewal Program as
well as in the other planning sections.7

Mr. Mitchell's relationship to the Planning
Commission and the Planning Department is very nebu-
lous.   He is rarely if ever seen by the Commission
and only occasionally by the staff, although his
diminishing role may not be of his own making.   As
to the Community Renewal Program itself, it is
difficult to discover what the approximately 80 non-
civil service members of this section are doing and
how the money, which is disbursed at the discretion
of the Chairman, is being used.   The Mitchell
consultant contract began on November 23, 1964 with
a sum of $350,000.   The total amount is now about
$8.4 million (including federal and city funds), an
increase of 700 percent since the present Chairman
took office in 1966.   Not only is the money used for
studies and salaries for the Community Renewal
Program but, apparently, much of it goes to other
sections within the Planning Department (Bronx Office,
Midtown Office, Urban Design Group).   The Chairman
recently acknowledged to a City Councilman that this
money may be used to get around civil service lines,
qualifications, salary schedules, and Bureau of the
Budget specifications.   This flexibility may at
times be positive, but such a large lump sum program
with so few visible results requires occasional

accountability. The federal government is about to
evaluate the entire multi-million dollar Community
Renewal Program; the results and recommendations of
this study will be extremely important to the City
of New York.

The Office of Comprehensive Planning is headed
by a Director, with Mr. Mitchell as consultant. The
program is funded by the City and the money is spent
at the discretion of the Chairman. The approximately
100-120 non-civil service staff members are totally
confused about their role and responsibilities.
Attempts to get studies under way are often rejected.
Contact between this staff and the Director is minimal. Supervision and direction are practically
nonexistent. The staff expresses the belief that it
is there to give the Planning Department the public
appearance of a large, functioning, professional
agency.*

Use of Consultants

Staff demoralization has increased with the
great emphasis on consultants. The present Chairman
relies to a considerable extent on outside consultants
(about 25 percent of the total agency budget, about
50 percent of individual planning offices). As of

-----

*The author informed the Deputy Mayor Richard
Avrelio, Comptroller Abraham Beame, and the Department
of Personnel of her findings. A recent request for
$5 million for the Community Renewal Program was
reduced to $313,000. The contract for the Compre-
hensive Planning Program was phased out in October,
1970. The Chairman has acquired a whole series of
civil service titles in an attempt to transfer over
non-civil service staff members originally hired
under the Mitchell consultant contract. Placing
such staff in civil service jobs at the same salaries
they received under the consultant contract will
give them salaries higher than those of the already
existing civil service lines on positions.

February, 1969, there were at least 21 consultant
contracts, not including the Mitchell contract and
contracts relating to the Master Plan. The designation
of consultants and the determination of the amount
of money to be spent and the studies to be conducted
are made predominantly by the Chairman. The staff
as well as the Commission are unaware of most of the
studies. The use of consultants is thought to be
good public relations because it carries with it an
aura of prestige and technical expertise as well as
a belief that the results must be good, and, therefore,
more acceptable. In fact, the studies may not be
any better than in-house studies and may be actually
inferior. Because of continual bypassing, the staff
is not motivated, not built up, and does not produce.
Therefore, the consultants must be used. Therefore,
the staff deteriorates, and so the cycle continues.
With most of the work done externally, there is no
staff--or Commission--commitment to the projects
and the programs may never be implemented. If the
Commission and staff were functioning together as
originally intended, an "In-House-Consultant Program"
could be initiated. Such a program would entail
continuous involvement of the Planning Department
staff, the Commission, the community, and the consultants, as needed. Working in-house would utilize
the professional capabilities of the staff and increase
the Planning Department's morale and efficiency.

In July-August, 1970, while the author was
writing these observations concerning the inordinate
use of consultants by the present City Planning
Department, a series of articles on the matter appeared
in The New York Times.[8] The articles questioned the
need for the great use of consultants, the quality
of input, substance, and result, and the impact on
the morale and work of the staff within City agencies.
The study of the City Planning Department in these
articles suggested that City Comptroller Abraham
Beame's analysis of the situation was correct: that
competent people were driven out because they were
bypassed or their work was given to consultants and
that "greater use should be made of our city employees
who have greater knowledge of city problems."[9] A
$300,000 Spring Creek consultant study approved by

the City Planning Commission was conducted by a
former junior planner in the City Planning Department
who had worked on a similar study within the planning
agency. A $150,000 consultant transportation study
of the Bronx reached the conclusion that "traffic
tends to move toward Manhattan in the morning and
away from Manhattan in the evening."[10]

The controversial series of articles continued
with the usual New York City histrionics. Councilman
Bertrand R. Gelfand stated that "It appears that the
City has developed a new industry called studying.
. . . Never before have we studied so much at such
a high cost and learned so little:" Mayor John V.
Lindsay issued a statement that "old fashioned,
encrusted municipal governments are not able to
modernize themselves from within"[11] and that critics
of the City's use of consultants were "anti-intel-
lectual."[12]

A Change in Staff Function

Due to the Chairman's close relationship with
the Mayor, he has been appointed to six other jobs
besides that of Chairman of the City Planning
Commission. With the changing role of the Chairman,
the role of the planning staff has changed. The
Chairman is also Chairman of the Mayor's Policy
Committee, formerly Chairman and now member of the
Model Cities Committee, member of the Metropolitan
Transportation Administration, member of the Tri-
State Commission, member of the United Nations
Development Corporation, and member of the Welfare
Island Development Corporation. Each of these positions, in and of itself, is more than a part-time job
As a result of the Chairman's involvement in all
these fields, the staff currently is more concerned
with operation, development, and execution than with
planning. Two side effects are the spreading thin
of staff efforts and the creation of conflict between
the regular City operating departments and the City
Planning Department and between the Commissioners
in the other City departments and the Chairman of
the City Planning Commission.

CONCLUSIONS

One may conclude that New York City is spending a great deal of money with minimal results. The amount of money spent is greater than ever before, the amount of staff turnover is greater than ever before, and the amount of production is less than ever before. The planning product is poor. Data-gathering is inadequate. Research, analysis, forecasting, and coordinating are practically nonexistent. There is continuous agency restructuring, reshuffling, and reassignment. No long-range development goals are established and decisions are on a project-by-project basis. Staff demoralization is at a peak. The Planning Department does not have the knowledge with which to perform its tasks, nor does it have leadership that understands the planning process. Planning has become political. It is ad hoc opportunism, directionless and dataless.

The impact of the present planning is nil in guiding the future development of the City. The public has lost confidence in the Planning Commission's ability and desire to deal with the economic, social, and physical problems of New York City. The dual nature of the agency, with the Planning Department separated from the Planning Commission, has resulted in a critical breakdown in the agency and a critical breakdown in planning.

The present commitment to planning can best be summed up by quoting from the proposed Master Plan: planning for the future is "intellectually presumptuous."[13]

Thus, it signals the "Death of Planning" for New York City.

NOTES

1. Editorial in The New York Times, July 11, 1970.

2. See T. J. Kent, Jr., The Urban General Plan (San Francisco: Chandler Publishing Co., 1964), p. 85.

3. Donald Elliott, "Memorandum," June 15, 1970

4. Communications Committee Recommendations (New York: City Planning Department Files, March, 1970).

5. Citizens Union, "Statement," 1970/71 Executive Budget Public Hearing, June 3, 1970.

6. William F. R. Ballard, "Memorandum, Transition Problems in re Executive Order No. 175" (New York: City Planning Commission, November 29, 1965), p. 5.

7. Series of Lectures, Community Renewal Program and Comprehensive Planning Program.

8. Martin Tolchin, "City Awarded $75 million in Contracts for Consulting Services in 1969 . . ." in The New York Times (Series of articles: July 1, 1969-July 17, 1970).

9. Tolchin, "Beame . . . Halts Payment to Consultant," op.cit. (July 3, 1970), p. 31.

10. Tolchin, "City Awarded $75 million in Contracts . . .," op.cit. (July 1, 1969), p. 41.

11. Tolchin, "Two Officials Score Consultant Pacts," op.cit. (July 2, 1970), p. 41.

12. Tolchin, "Beame . . . Halts payment to Consultant," op.cit. (July 3, 1970), p. 31.

13. New York City Planning Commission, Plan for New York City, 1969, A Proposal, Vol. 1 (New York: Dept. of City Planning), p. 6.

4

THE

COMPREHENSIVE

PLAN

> The need for vision of the future in the
> governance of cities has not lessened
> with the years. The dweller within the
> gates, even more than the stranger from
> afar, will pay the price of blindness.[1]

To determine the effectiveness of an independent city planning commission, it is necessary to evaluate the planning product. In New York City, the major responsibilities of the Planning Commission are comprehensive planning, functional planning, capital budgeting, and zoning.

According to the New York City Charter "the City Planning Commission shall prepare and adopt in one or more parts, and from time to time modify, a master plan for the physical development of the City, which shall provide for the improvement of the City and its future growth."[2] The Master Plan is approved solely by the Planning Commission, after public hearings, and serves merely as advisory to the Mayor and the City Council. It does not, in other words, have the power of an official act.

However, federal legislation providing for financial aid for urban renewal, housing, and other capital improvements consistently requires that such projects be in accord with the Master Plan. New York

State's Enabling Zoning Law requires that zoning regulations be "in accord with a well considered plan."[3]

Under the Chairmanship of Rexford Tugwell, individual plans for specific kinds of development were initiated. Between 1940 and 1963, ten such plans were approved by the City Planning Commission:

1. Master Plan of Sections Containing Areas for Development and Redevelopment, January 3, 1940

2. Master Plan of Schools, January 22, 1941

3. Master Plan of Sewage Treatment Plant Sites and Tributary Areas, April 16, 1941

4. Master Plan of Health Center Districts and Facilities, November 3, 1943

5. Master Plan of Arterial Highways and Major Streets, April 11, 1945, superseding a Master Plan of a System of Express Highways, Parkways, and Major Streets, January 22, 1941

6. Master Plan of the Brooklyn Civic Center, May 8, 1945

7. Master Plan of Sanitation Facilities, November 21, 1945

8. Master Plan of Major Airports, December 19, 1945

9. Master Plan of Parks, May 3, 1961

10. Master Plan of New York Civic Center, April 18, 1963.

In or about 1965, Mayor Robert F. Wagner directed Planning Commission Chairman William F. R. Ballard to initiate the preparation of a Comprehensive Master Plan for the City. Work began almost immediately. Mr. Ballard was replaced in November, 1966, by a new Chairman, Donald H. Elliott. The Master Plan

was not a high priority item for the new Chairman
and the work lagged. However, the City was under
pressure from Washington to produce its Master Plan.
Active work resumed approximately in the winter of
1968. On November 14, 1969, the Planning Commission
presented its proposed Master Plan, which consists
of six volumes, one for each borough and one entitled
"Critical Issues."

A CRITIQUE OF THE MASTER PLAN

Professional and public response to the Master
Plan has been almost universally critical of its
substance, its manner of production, and its presentation. It has been criticized on various levels by:

Regional Plan Association
The New York Metropolitan Chapter of the
   American Institute of Planners
The City Club
The Metropolitan Section of the American
   Society of Civil Engineers
Citizens Union
Planners for Equal Opportunity
The Village Voice
Dr. Kenneth Clark, President of the Metro-
   politan Applied Research Corporation
Roger Starr, Executive Director of the
   Citizens' Housing and Planning Council
Edward Logue of the New York Urban Develop-
   ment Corporation
Wolf Von Eckhardt, architect, and by many
   others.[4]

To understand the problem of the Master Plan
and the ensuing negative public reaction, it would
be well to consider the movie that was to introduce
the Master Plan. The title of the movie, "What Is
The City But The People," were words spoken by the
tribune Sicinius in William Shakespeare's Tragedy of
Coriolanus. The tragedy of Coriolanus is the tragedy
of the movie and of the Master Plan. Coriolanus'
tragedy was hubris, pride: the inability to understand,
to relate to, or to consult with the common people

and give them true participation. For all his good
words, Coriolanus could only identify with and plan
for his own elite class. "Had Coriolanus but a sense
of humility, disaster could have been avoided."
When one views the movie, one is struck with a similar
sense of arrogance and disdain for the people. The
movie states that the ghetto streets are dirty
because of the people who inhabit them and then shows
upper-income brownstones, all clean and filled with
beautiful white people, who incidentally may think
about sending their children to public schools.
Tall New York City buildings with dynamic headquarters
activities and executives from Des Moines, Iowa, or
Stamford, Connecticut, are truly praised; while those
dislocated for the elegant buildings are merely dislocated. The Puerto Rican man is told if he works
hard by day, goes to school at night, and keeps his
apartment clean, he too may get ahead. And the star
of the movie, the Chairman of the Planning Commission,
walks majestically through "his" city.

If having a decent and professional planning
process in New York City were not so important, the
whole business of the Master Plan could be enjoyed
as one grand farce. With respect to the production
of the Master Plan, for example, the full Planning
Commission met briefly in April, 1967, for one and
one-half days in the summer of 1967, for two days
in the summer of 1968, and for two hours in 1969--
this was the total involvement of the full Commission
in regard to the Master Plan. As galley proofs
became available, Commissioners were "allowed" to
see them, one section at a time, to be returned
in three working days. The sections were printed
with red ink on black paper so that they could not
be xeroxed.

The Planning Department staff's participation
was also minimal. Staff members were denied their
requests to make suggestions for revision and did
not see the document until it was presented to the
public.

While the Master Plan sings loud paeans to
citizen participation, the fact is that citizens,

civic groups, business associations, local planning
boards, other City departments, officials, and
legislators did not participate in its making. The
Master Plan is solely the result of the intuitive
decisions made by the authors;* it reflects their
values and judgments rather than the needs, values,
and preferences of the people of the City.

Incredibly, the Master Plan's authors label
goal formation, forecasting, the adoption of standards,
abstracting cause and effect relationships, and
analyzing the consequences of alternative actions as
"paper boldness and intellectually presumptious."[5]
Instead, the authors advocate "a step-by-step process
that will allow us and our successors to adapt to
the unforeseen."[6] The Master Plan deals with feel-
ings, attitudes, promises, and hopes; it avoids any
clearcut policies to guide the City's future growth.
Small wonder that the Metropolitan Chapter of the
American Institute of Planners concluded that "the
Plan as presented must be deemed harmful to the
people of the City . . . and to the further development of urban planning in the United States."[7]

Intuition alone is not sufficient for writing
a Master Plan. The Master Plan presented is merely
a synthesis of much traveled ideas and vague, glib
generalities. Under the guise of presenting a new
type of plan, a social plan, the Planning Commission
fails to state or even understand the interrelationship between physical planning and social planning.
Physical programs are devised to achieve social
goals; the two are mutually supportive. They tell
us what are our goals, where we are going, and how
we will get there.

---

*Apparently, the authors were the Chairman and
a few close associates. Much of the writing was
done by editor-journalist-writer William Whyte.
However, the Master Plan is presented as a Planning
Commission document.

Three major assumptions govern the thinking of the authors of the Master Plan: (1) that the critical issue is the growth of the National Center, which will provide sufficient revenue to pay for improved municipal services and remedial services to upgrade the blighted areas and provide adequate programs to equip people for jobs; (2) that citizen demand for broad distribution of public services should be given lower priority than meeting the needs of a small fraction of the population--the Commission believes that these people have an invigorating influence on the character of the City, out of all proportion to numbers; and (3) that the problems of New York City must be solved within New York City-- that we can create enough land, space, housing, and jobs to provide all the people with a decent environment.

A public policy based on these assumptions will not even begin to attack the problems of middle- and low-income people--the problems of poverty, race, joblessness, homelessness, and inequality. The Master Plan's basic assumption that the National Center is the critical issue is not a valid assumption for three reasons: (1) it has no relation to the majority of people living within the City; (2) the emphasis on the National Center is detrimental to the development of subcenters in the rest of the region; and (3) increased concentration in the Central Business District will be self-defeating in the long run.

The National Center is merely a new gilded phrase for the same old urban renewal. Whatever the nomenclature, it means the same downtown renewal, the same neglect of other parts of the City. In the past, this discredited policy not only failed to save the cities but also served to isolate and segregate the poor.[8] For example, despite the fact that New York City has built about 30 million square feet of office space in Manhattan in the past five years, welfare costs have tripled and more than one million people are on welfare.*

_____

*Square feet of office space built in 1969 was

The Master Plan gives respectability to the
systematic maximization of land values in Manhattan
and the concomitant emptying out of industry, manu-
facturing, marginal commercial activities, and the
low- and moderate-income people now residing in the
borough, a process by which Manhattan is recreated
into an island unto itself for the select few to
live and work. This is the Planning Commission's
goal and the "critical issue." Such a goal only
increases the distance between two societies. The
rest of the City outside Manhattan, the rest of the
people, are left to their own resources to live out
their lives in an unplanned, and uncontrolled at-
mosphere.

The Planning Commission prefers to allocate its
resources and commitment to Manhattan. In actuality,
the maximization of Manhattan may prove disastrous.
Twenty years hence, the City may not be able to sus-
tain the concentration. The City will create a
supersaturated solution whereby the headquarters
activity will be forced to precipitate out. With
technological advances, automation, and computer-
ization, headquarters activity need not stay in the
City. With problems of crime, congestion, pollution,
housing shortages, transportation, and communication,
it will be counter to the principle of natural ad-
vantage for such activity to remain. Headquarters
activity is important to Manhattan, but judgments
concerning critical issues for the City's future
must be based on valid assumptions and hard facts.

The Master Plan states that increased concentration is the "genius" of the City--the "engine."
In its infatuation with engines, the Commission
fails to understand that engines may be inefficient,
wear out, cause pollution, and at times be engines

9,958,000, 1970 was 13,524,000, and 1971 is estimated
at 28,766,000 (figures from Planning Department,
Manhattan Office). In the 1970/71 budget, there
was a $60 million increase over estimated costs for
welfare (Bureau of the Budget).

of destruction. The Commission has made no technical
studies concerning the need for concentration and
its impact on people and behavior. The Master Plan
entirely ignores the implications of such concentration the City's already overstrained transport system
and the City's ability to service high density. The
City's delivery system is presently malfunctioning.
The Mayor's Midtown Planning and Development Office
claims that the infrastructure within the midtown
area has passed the margin of safety.* Increased
concentration can only prove to be a destructive
element, crippling growth and wasting public and
private investment. What the Commission should be
concerned with is not the quantity of lives but the
quality of life.

The Planning Commission's proposed Master Plan
isolates and insulates the City and is totally lacking
in a regional concept. The Commission has little
understanding of urbanization and the City's role
and relationship to the larger urban area. Statistics
show that the population of metropolitan areas is
increasing while that of central cities is decreasing.
Although 94.5 percent of the American people live
in urban areas, the flow of population is to the
suburban areas and not to the central cities. The
resulting geographic, economic, and social inter-
dependence of the metropolitan area has created
problems that can be resolved only on a regional
basis. At the 46th Annual Convention of the National
League of Cities, Dr. Philip M. Hauser stated that
the United States has changed so fast from a rural
to an urban society that the attitudes of its citizens
have not kept pace: "The dead hand of the past
imposes itself on contemporary society, and government

---

*A Regional Plan Association News Release on
The Master Plan ("City Should Concentrate on Bringing
Offices to Downtown Brooklyn, Jamaica. . . .," September
9, 1970, p. 1) stated that "City services, transportation, telephones and nearby housing simply aren't
keeping up with the needs of increasing office workers
in Manhattan."

is still mired in the eighteenth and nineteenth centuries."[9] Surely, the New York City Planning Commission should think and plan in terms of the twentieth century, if not the twenty-first, and set goals of improving the quality of life within the City.

CONCLUSIONS

The experience with the Master Plan reveals the fundamental lack of professionalism at the center of the planning operation in New York City. If the Chairman and his confidantes understand the discipline of process, they ignore it. If they understand research, they avoid it. Participation in the planning process either frightens or confuses them.

Structural changes in the planning system offer no guarantee that the cavalier style attending the production of the Master Plan would change, but it would at least raise up the opportunity for administrative changes and, hopefully, for the infusion of professionalism. For in the Master Plan, to quote Socrates, "our conversation is not about something casual, but about the proper way to live."

NOTES

1. Hesse v. Rath, 249 N.Y. 436, 164 N.E. 342

2. New York City Charter, adopted November 7, 1961 effective January 1, 1963, Sec. 197b., c., Sec. 199, pursuant to General City Law, Chap. 21 of the Consolidated Laws of New York State, Art. 3, Sec. 28a.

3. General City Law, Chap. 21 of the Consolidated Laws of New York State, Art. 2-A, Sec. 25.

4. See Beverly Moss Spatt, "Dissenting Report, Plan for New York City," published with the "Master Plan" by the New York City Planning Commission (Vol.I, 1969).

5.   New York City Planning Commission, "Plan for New York City, 1969, A Proposal," Vol. I (New York: Dept. of City Planning, 1969), p. 6.

6.   Ibid.

7.   New York Chapter, American Institute of Planners, "Early Draft" (New York, June, 1970), p. 1.

8.   Paul N. Ylvisaker discusses the need to consider other methods than urban renewal to renew the City: "We have placed the Ford Foundation's first bet not on the central business district of the city, but on its school system, . . . on the City and metropolitan area's employment system, on their administration of justice, and a growing list of similarly critical 'production processes' . . ." From an address in January, 1963 entitled "Community Action: A Response to Some Unfinished Business," found in Daniel P. Moynihan, Maximum Feasible Misunderstanding: Community Action in the War on Poverty, (New York: The Free Press, 1969).

9.   John Herbers, "Nation's Urban Officials Foretell . . .," The New York Times, December 6, 1969.

5

THE

FUNCTIONAL PLAN:

HOUSING

Planning relates to all aspects of urban life.
In evaluating the City Planning Commission, it is
necessary to determine whether or not the present
planning process is assuring the achievement of
functional objectives in a rational manner. Planning
is germane to a housing policy. Land allocation,
space, community facilities, circulation patterns,
and timing are important concerns of housing and
planning. The Planning Commission is legally responsible for the development of an overall articulated
housing program--born out of knowledge, nursed in
community dialogue, holistic in view, adequate in
number. The City Charter charges the Planning Commission with the formulation of a Master Plan for
the City that shall "afford adequate and appropriate
facilities for the housing . . . of its population."[1]

The Planning Commission's role in zoning, mapping,
capital budgeting, designation of urban renewal areas,
and approval of public and publicly-assisted housing
enables the Commission to control future housing
development.[2] In addition, the Chairman of the
Planning Commission exerts influence on housing
policies through his membership on the Site Selection
Board[3] and the Mayor's Policy Committee.

PRESCRIPTIVE SCOPE

Planning for housing programs includes a variety of programs beyond that of merely building housing units. Urban planners have within their prescriptive scope planning for auxiliary facilities and services for housing, building regulations and enforcement programs, housing subsidies, rent control, maintenanc rehabilitation, conservation, zoning, relocation, and administrative organizations and mechanisms. Planner are concerned with the physical, social, and economic totality. In 1967, the American Institute of Planner repealed Article II of its Constitution and substitut "unified" and comprehensive planning for "land use" determination. Also in 1967, the federal Bureau of the Budget wrote the requirement for comprehensive planning into its guidelines for eligibility for federal assistance. Thus, total planning has been given legal status.[4]

CURRENT ENVIRONMENT

New York City is a municipality consisting of five boroughs--Manhattan, Bronx, Brooklyn, Queens, and Richmond--and a population of 7.9 million. It is the central city of a metropolitan area of 8,000 square miles and 1,400 units of government.

There are a total of 2,987,300 housing units within New York City. Of these units, 73 percent are in multi-family structures, 11 percent in Old-Law tenements (built prior to 1901) and 96,000 are rooming houses with shared facilities. Of the housin inventory, about 250,000 units were built with some form of public assistance--144,300 are public housing units and 108,700 are publicly-assisted private housing units.[5]

Currently, New York City is characterized by an inadequate housing supply, a lack of housing choice, a great amount of substandard housing, increasing abandonment, a mismatching of housing and job oppor-tunities, inadequate relocation resources, and

overcrowded conditions. Added to these problems is
the fact that publicly-assisted housing cannot be
produced at rentals low enough for low- and moderate-
income people. The inadequacy of housing for low-
and middle-income families gives rise to two significant problems. First, the housing inventory is
incapable of matching the need for new dwelling
units created by the formation of new households and
the requirements of deteriorated housing. Second,
the inadequacy of the housing stock is continuing
the existence of slum areas and racial segregation.

According to the Regional Plan Association
there is an immediate need for a 50 percent annual
increase in new housing construction. The housing
needs for 1960-85 include 1,175,000 additional dwelling units--961,000 for replacement or rehabilitation
and the remainder for new households. The annual
rate of production in 1960-85 must be a minimum of
48,050 units.[6]

In 1967, there were 23,000 completions--10,000
publicly-aided units and 13,000 private dwelling
units--while 6,000 dwelling units were demolished.
In 1968, a total of only 20,000 units were built,
privately financed as well as publicly-aided. Of
these, 9,930 units were for low- and middle-income
families.[7]

The 1969 housing program was a total failure
that reflected the absence of any realistic planning.
Although the Lindsay administration proclaimed that
1969 would constitute the most energetic, comprehensive
housing program in the history of this city, the
fact is that 1969 constituted one of the worst years
in the history of housing production. The total
number of low- and middle-income dwelling units in
construction was 8,633--two-thirds in new construction
and one-third in rehabilitation. Of these 8,633
dwelling units, 1,949 were low-income units. This
figure is particularly disastrous in light of the
fact that there are over 135,000 low-income families
on the public housing waiting list, that 450-500,000
households cannot find housing of size and rental
appropriate to meet their needs, that 276,000 dwelling

units are occupied by families with an annual income
below $3,000, that there are 800,000 existing sub-
standard units, that over 50,000 families live in
housing that is substandard due to overcrowding,
that nearly one-half of all one-room dwelling units
are substandard, that over 30,000 dwelling units a
year are being abandoned (100,000 in the three years
1966-68), and that between 1965 and 1968 there was
a net loss of dwelling units.

Of the 7,822 low- and middle-income dwelling
units put into construction in 1969, 3,292 were
middle-income units; however most of these "middle-
income" units will be coming in at rentals that
middle-income people cannot afford. In 1969, buildin
permits in the private finance field, dwindled to a
paltry 3,000 dwelling units.[8]

According to the Housing and Development Administration, in the first 9 months of 1970, there were
6,927 government-aided low- and middle-income dwellin
units put into construction(starts), of which number
1,826 were public housing units.*

-----

*These figures are based on an official presen-
tation to the Planning Commission by Robert Hagen of
the Housing and Development Administration, on submission of the Capital Budget Request for 1971/72.
According to the New York Times (Steven R. Weisman,
"City-Aided Housing Starts . . .," January 13, 1971,
p. 18), the Mayor estimated 17,899 city-aided starts
for 1970. A close analysis of this figure reveals
the inclusion of 3,335 rehabilitated units and 4,586
units of which 1,540 have been counted in previous
years and 3,046 which have not been started as of
December 31, 1970. Therefore, the total of new
construction starts for 1970 (12 months), using the
administration's figures, comes to 9,978 dwelling
units. Included in this count are also about 3,370
of 6,521 state-aided units. The total amount of
city-aided starts would be 6,608 units.

Another example of the inadequate accounting

It may be concluded that the critical housing shortage is becoming worse. At the present rate of construction it would take over 80 years merely to replace the 800,000 substandard units that currently exist. Contributing to the problem are suburban zoning restrictions and other external social and economic factors. Black and Puerto Rican families are moving into New York City in large numbers. During the years 1951-65, 640,000 black and Puerto Rican people moved into the City. Fifteen years hence, the City's black and Puerto Rican population may be 4,000,000--one-half of the total population. (This figure includes immigration and natural increases.) If the housing trend continues, these groups with lower than average incomes will occupy the least adequate and least expensive dwelling units in racially segregated areas. In 1960, 62 percent of the housing units in the City cost less than $100 monthly and 78 percent of black and Puerto Rican households occupied such units.[9]

PROSPECTIVE ENVIRONMENT

In 1967, Jason Nathan stated that with reorganization and establishment of the superagency, Housing and Development Administration, new programs, faster service, and completion of imaginative new projects would follow and the City would soon come much nearer to its goal.[10] By 1970, he apparently had changed his mind. Speaking before the New York State Housing Committee, he said, "Crisis may well be the most overworked word in the English language when the

---

procedure is the administration's estimate of 13,178 completions in 1970. An analysis of this figure reveals that included in this count are 6,019 state Mitchell-Lama units not completed and nearly 3,000 rehabilitated units. The total of new completions for 1970 thus comes to 4,689 dwelling units.

Whatever the exact figures, they are insufficient in light of the grave social need.

cities are talked about. But it is no exaggeration
if the subject is housing, crisis is an understate-
ment. Disaster may be more appropriate."[11]

In discussing future housing construction,
Manhattan Borough President Percy Sutton "lamented
bureaucratic delay resulting from a lack of over-all
planning."[12]

The City Planning Department many times has
spoken of the need for a unified program to gain
flexibility in providing additional dwelling units
and called for a "comprehensive plan as a tool for
action."[13] With the housing situation so acute,
there is little political interest in a plan for a
long-range period--the desire is for action now.
Yet immediate action is thwarted by a series of
conflicts. Whereas federal legislation mandates and
the political situation necessitates community partici
pation in planning, this very participation results
in great delays, increased costs, and often unreal-
ized housing units. Not only is conflict rampant
within the communities, but conflict also exists
among planners and officials on choosing between the
economic goal of maximizing the land value and the
social goal of achieving and maintaining housing
units for low- and moderate-income people. (Manhattan
Borough President Percy Sutton, frequently has expressed concern that Manhattan will become a home
for the very rich and the very poor.)

The prospective environment is made more complex
by the difficulty of autonomous forecasting. Housing
is dependent upon such factors as interest rates,
construction costs, real estate taxes, union contracts
and practices, and federal legislation and appropria-
tions. Public housing in New York City is contingent
upon a higher limitation on room costs. The Model
Cities Program is dependent upon adequate allocations,
but these allocations cannot be predetermined. The
end of inflation is indeterminate. The relaxation
of union practices and the opening up of membership
to minority people remain in doubt.

An important environmental factor is the political

unit. New York City has no control over the policies
of the 1,400 political jurisdictions in the New York
Metropolitan Region, although New York's housing
problems can be solved only on an area-wide basis.

An indication of the absence of any overall City
plan for future housing may be seen in the current
Master Plan. The Master Plan clearly shows a lack
of comprehension and scope.   The Lindsay administration has stated that the success of government hinges
on a commitment to a planning approach. Yet the
product of the Planning Commission is the very denial
of a housing commitment and the denial of any clear
set of objectives, policies, or overall development
strategies. The Master Plan programs the clearance
of only 10,000 dwelling units per year and continues
the rehabilitation of thousands of unfit units despite
the fact that experience has shown that such units
cannot be adequately rehabilitated and that the cost
of their rehabilitation approximates that of new construction. The Master Plan makes no provision for
continued deterioration, although the preamble mentions
the "probable" need for the City to take over the
ever-growing number of thousands of units being abandoned by their owners. Nowhere does the Planning
Commission address itself to its commitment to the
national goal of six million low- and middle-income
units over a period of ten years. The Plan's programmed rate of construction of 28,000 low- and
middle-income units per year is grossly inadequate.
If the City really desires to provide for the well-
being of the citizens, if the City is going to close
the rare gap, if a social catastrophe is to be avoided,
the City must create a rational achievable housing
plan. Only when there is an adequate supply of housing
will the inexorable demand of the housing market contribute to freedom of choice whereby the City residents
may move to decent dwelling units according to their
economic ability and social taste.[14]

SCATTERED-SITE, VEST POCKET PUBLIC HOUSING

In order to comply with the new regulations
promulgated by the United States Department of Housing

and Urban Development and to achieve racial and
economic integration throughout the City, the Lindsay
administration and the City Planning Commission instituted the scattered-site, vest pocket public housing
program--the placing of small projects on vacant lots
in stable middle-income communities. This important
program has been a total failure because of the
absence of any planning input, coordination, or
rationale. The vacant site was the common denominator
of all the proposals. The existence of a vacant site
cannot be the sole determinant for a housing project,
nor can it, by itself, create economic integration.
Many of the projects were large projects, inappropri-
ate in size in terms of the community. In fact, many
were isolated from the main communities, residents,
and facilities. The recital of community facilities
was more often a facade, a quantitative list with no
qualitative judgment. Most of the proposals smacked
of the same old approach that had failed so dramati-
cally elsewhere.

The units and the need for public housing can
be justified, the approach cannot. The City has an
obligation to plan for appropriate sites and not to
search desperately for vacant sites and then prepare
a rationale to justify a poor selection.* Such a
program will not provide economic or ethnic integration, nor will it provide a suitable residential
environment with all the necessary supporting facilities. The Planning Commission must explore skillfully
and energetically new techniques and new approaches
and not use the same tired techniques with new seman-
tics. The Commission has the responsibility to con-
front the reality and enormity of the housing situatic

----

*In March, 1966, Mayor Lindsay created the
Special Interagency Committee on Housing. Edward
Robin, now acting Executive Director of the City
Planning Department (then assistant to Donald H.
Elliott, who was then Counsel to the Mayor), was
appointed Housing Coordinator of the Committee. As
such, he had major responsibility for the selection
of these sites.

and come up with an achievable low-rental program.
Scattered-site housing must be planned so that it
becomes the positive instrument by which the low-
income family moves into a new neighborhood, benefits
from the new environment, and at the same time is of
benefit to the established community.

A scattered-site housing program requires not
only intelligent planning but also administrative
skill on the part of the Commission in selling this
program to the neighborhood residents and the Borough
Presidents. Citizens' Housing and Planning Council
questions "the skill with which this policy has been
advanced. The success . . . depends on two missing
ingredients. The first of these is the political
talent to make these site selections acceptable to
present residents. Clearly, low-rent developments
will never be fully acceptable to all of the people
who live near a proposed site and feel that the City
is undermining the value of their homes. Skillfull
negotiation and persuasion might, however, reduce the
fear that makes this prophecy self-fulfilling." The
Council also notes that "in any such persuasion, the
Borough Presidents play a key role," yet "Mr. Lindsay
and his colleagues seem very reluctant to enter into
such discussions with the Borough Presidents. They
prefer to stand on high moral ground, on which negotiations are difficult to arrange." The second missing
ingredient is planning for necessary supporting
facilities. The Council speaks to the "difficulty
the Administration is encountering in arranging for
construction of public facilities to accompany
housing developments."[15]

Many civic groups support the scattered-site
housing program but with the condition that the City,
in each case, consider "good planning to insure the
suitability of such housing for neighborhood development."[16]

The result of this impoverished plan, in terms
of completions, is zero. Five years after approval,
only one project is certain to be built (Cassidy
Place, Staten Island). This disaster does not negate
the concept of scattered-site public housing but it

does show the need for a deep commitment to planning
for such a program. Planning for such a sensitive
program requires "patience, care, and a measure of
humility in the face of as difficult a set of social
questions as urban men have ever tried to solve
peacefully by the application of their conscious
will."[17]

MIDDLE-INCOME HOUSING

On December 23, 1968, Mayor Lindsay broke ground
for six Mitchell-Lama middle-income housing projects
and stated that "an all-time record" for starts of
such projects would be set in 1969.[18] What the Mayor
failed to say was that the majority of these units
would be too expensive for middle-income people to
occupy. The middle-income projects to which he
referred would be coming in predominantly at $50-60
per room per month, bringing an average two-bedroom
apartment to as much as $300 per month--suitable for
families with annual incomes of $25,000. (Mitchell-
Lama projects presently before the Board of Estimate
are projected at $75 per room per month; Waterside
[CP 21235] will cost $87.42 per room per month.)
The skewing of rents to provide the mandated reserva-
tion of 20 percent of the units for low-income familie
will further increase the average rent, permitting
families with annual incomes of $30,000 to occupy
these middle-income, publicly-aided units.*

---

*The author publicly recommended (CP19898, Octobe
18, 1967) legislation mandating that all publicly-
aided, middle-income housing have an adequate percent-
age of low-rental units. Subsequently, the Housing
and Development Administration issued an executive
order that 20 percent of such units be allocated to
low-rental units. After an in-depth study of City
Mitchell-Lama projects, it may be concluded that the
achievement of this mandate is in question, that the
skewing to achieve the low-rental units is further
exacerbating the situation, and that the number of
low-rental units will amount to a paltry few.

The families for whom these units are being
planned are not of middle income. The 1969 Annual
Report of the President's Council on Economic Advisors
stated that the national average family income in
1967 was $7,974. A City University of New York
survey estimated that the median income in New York
City in 1966 was $6,684.[19] The 1960 United States
Census indicated that 95 percent of the American
people earned under $15,000 per year. Most of New
York City's middle-income starts will be unattainable
for 95 percent of the population--that is, they will
be geared to 5 percent of the people. The intent of
the Mitchell-Lama legislation is to provide dwelling
units for those whose incomes are too high for public
housing and too low to compete in the private market.
In actuality, the City is using this legislation to
grant an up to 84 percent tax abatement and a 90
percent City mortgage for high-income housing.
Public subsidies are actually being used for the
lowest priority group. This perversion of the middle-
income legislation began with the City Planning
Commission's proposal for Waterside (at $53.01 per
room per month)* and continued with Chelsea Walk
($60 per room per month) and Ruppert Brewery ($60
per room per month). Dissenting reports on these
proposals stated that it was time for the Planning
Commission to publicly articulate the fact that the
Mitchell-Lama program was not producing units for
middle-income families; that new techniques and aids
(such as interest rate subsidies, capital cost write-
downs, and rent supplements) were needed to bring
the rentals down to middle-income levels; and that
these aids must be applied within the context of a
specific overall plan for public and private housing.[20]

Donald H. Elliott, Chairman of the City Planning
Commission, has continued to praise the Mitchell-Lama
program, contending that middle income was now very

---

*Waterside was first submitted as a Redevelopment
Companies Law Project. It is now being resubmitted
as a Limited Profit Housing Corporation Law Project
(June, 1970, CP 21235).

broadly defined. This contention is contrary to the
Planning Commission's own 1965 and 1968 Community
Renewal Reports, which stated that government should
avoid subsidizing housing that rents above a moderate
rent level and that the subsidized housing program
must "strike close to the heart of the problem."21

CONCLUSIONS

Development of a public policy, plan, and program
is a government responsibility. Citizens may recom-
mend and advise; government must perform. The issue
that clearly emerges is whether the Planning Commission moves step by step without an adequate knowledge
of total needs or whether the steps are to be taken
in context of a meaningful development plan within
which urban growth may take place. The present
planning agency has produced no housing plan. It
spills more words and produces less accomplishments:

What purports to be a housing plan and
program is a series of ad hoc decisions
generally made in impetuous haste to meet
either impending deadlines or community
and political pressures. Nowhere in the
housing program are the comprehensive and
cohesive policies and plans necessary to
renew the City's housing stock and to
provide every New York citizen with sound
housing in a sound community.22

NOTES

1. New York City Charter, adopted November 7,
1961, effective January 1, 1963, Chap. 8, Sec. 197a,
Pursuant to General City Law, Chap. 21 of the Consolidated Laws of New York State, Art. 3, Sec. 28a.

2. New York City Charter, adopted November 7,
1961, effective January 1, 1963, Chaps. 8 and 9,
pursuant to Planning and Zoning Enabling Laws, General
City Law, Chap. 21, Consolidated Laws of New York
State, Art. 3, Sec. 26-39; Art. 2-A, Sec. 20; Art.
5-A, Sec. 81-83, 99-g.

The City Planning Commission may designate an area
suitable for Urban Renewal and include recommendations
for action, after a public hearing (General Municipal
Law, Consolidated Laws of New York State, Art. 15,
Sec. 504). Formal public notice is by publication in
the Calendar of the City Planning Commission and the
City Record for ten days prior to the public hearing.

The City Planning Commission shall hold a public
hearing on an Urban Renewal Plan and if approved the
Plan goes to The Board of Estimate for final approval
(Ibid., Sec. 505[2]).

The City Planning Commission may approve middle-
income sites and projects under Mitchell-Lama legislation ("Limited Profit Housing Companies Act," #10
et seq., Art. II of the New York State Private Housing
Finance Law; and "Redevelopment Companies Act," #100
et seq., Art. III of the New York State Private
Housing Finance Law.

The City Planning Commission may approve a public
housing project (#150, New York State Public Housing
Law). Public hearings are not mandated by State
law but held pursuant to City Planning Commission
practice.

The delegation of powers in the area of housing is
pursuant to Article XVIII, New York State Constitution.

Federal Title I aid is pursuant to General Municipal
Law, op. cit. Federally assisted Sec. 221 (D) 3 and
Sec. 236 are reviewed only by the City Planning
Commission if City assistance is given pursuant to
State housing laws, op. cit.

(All plans and projects are submitted informally to
the City Planning Commission for general approval.
If a preliminary acceptability is indicated, detailed
formal plans are devised and submitted.)

     3. New York City Charter, adopted November 7,
1961, effective January 1, 1963, Chap. 9, Sec. 227.

4.   Willard Hansen, "The Expanding Prescriptive Scope of Area-Wide Planning" (New York University, Course Lecture Notes: Fall, 1969), p. 11.

5.   Committee on Housing Statistics, "Housing Statistic Handbook" (New York, October, 1968).   The January, 1970, figure for public housing units is 151,000.

6.   These figures are based on the Regional Plan Association "Housing Opportunities," Regional Plan News, 91 (September, 1969).   Since the latest figures show a significant decrease in the rate of new construction and a net decrease in the housing stock, the rate of increase required must be even greater than that stated in the Regional Plan Association study.

7.   New York City Housing and Development Administration files, 1969.

8.   New York City, Building Department files, 1969.

9.   Regional Plan Association, op. cit.

10.   Jason Nathan, "Speech" given at Town Meeting of the League of Women Voters of the City of New York on January 12, 1968, in Active Voter (League of Women Voters of the City of New York, February, 1968), 3.

11.   Jason Nathan, "Statement on New York City Housing," in Discussion Outline (League of Women Voters of the City of New York, March 17, 1970).

12.   Percy Sutton, "Speech" given at Town Meeting of League of Women Voters of the City of New York on January 12, 1968, in Active Voter (League of Women Voters of the City of New York, February, 1968).

13.   New York City Department of City Planning, Newsletter (July-August, 1967).

14.   See Beverly Moss Spatt, "Dissenting Report, Plan for New York City," published with the "Master

Plan" by the New York City Planning Commission (Vol. I, 1969).

15.   Citizens' Housing and Planning Council, Housing and Planning News, XXVI, 4-5 (January-February, 1968), 2.

16.   League of Women Voters of the City of New York, "Consensus of New York City's Housing Program" (February, 1969).

17.   Citizens' Housing and Planning Council, Housing and Planning News, XXIV, 7 (June, 1966), 3.

18.   Joseph P. Fried, "Record Year Seen for City Housing," The New York Times, December 24, 1968.

19.   Donald G. Hay and M. J. Wantman, Estimates of Population Characteristics, New York City--1964-1965-1966, (New York: The City University of New York, RB-P4-68, June, 1968), p. 15.

20.   Beverly Moss Spatt, "Dissenting Report" CP-19664,5,6,7,8 (New York: City Planning Commission, April 12, 1967) and "Dissenting Report" CP-20197, (New York: City Planning Commission, March 20, 1968).

21.   Community Renewal Program, "New York City's Renewal Strategy, 1965" (New York: City Planning Commission, December, 1965), p. 44.   (Revised Edition: 1968.)

22.   Edwin Friedman, "Letter to the Editor," The New York Times, January, 1969.

6

THE ROLE OF THE CITY
PLANNING COMMISSION

To understand the City Planning Commission's role in capital budgeting, one must go back a bit in history. The planning function was established in the 1936 New York City Charter[1] as a corrective to the purely political determination of City development policies. These corrective measures were to be provided by two major steps: (1) the preparation and public presentation of an objective view of facts and values by which development and construction could be judged and (2) the establishment of public hearings through which all measures relating to City development policy could be brought to the open forum of public discussion, where different interest groups might present their concerns and reactions. Thus, an evaluation of the City Planning Commission must be made against this background, viewed as to whether the present agency is meeting the two aforementioned criteria: (1) whether it is enhancing or diminishing public discussion and information about alternatives and implications and (2) whether or not it is substituting purely political judgments for judgments based on technical information and knowledge.

Whether or not the Capital Budget is prepared by the Planning Commission, the Mayor is going to put his impress on it in terms of programs and policies that he favors. This is a proper procedure and an exercise of office and power for which he is elected. But the fact remains that, however good the Mayor, he has neither the knowledge nor the time to make the determinations for most of the Capital Budget and consequently must rely on his advisors. Thus, much depends on the nature, functions, and quality of his advisors. Fundamentally, there are two questions:

1. Does it make a difference to have the Capital Budget prepared by the City Planning Commission?

2. Does it make a difference if the City Planning Commission's public hearings are discontinued

Should the Planning Commission Prepare the Capital Budget?

The Capital Budget is a major tool for realizatio of the Master Plan. The City Planning Commission is responsible for the creation of a Master Plan, a policy for City development. Since the proposed Master Plan is more a political statement than a planning document and sets no guidelines for the future development of the City, it cannot be used as a framework against which to judge developmental decisions and public improvements.*

Capital Budget-making requires planning competence. The City Planning Department does not have personnel trained in the particular analytical and technical perspectives that should be brought to bear on project evaluation, value judgments, and recommendations, nor does it have the necessary informational background. The Department lacks

------

*The 1970/71 and 1971/72 Capital Budgets were prepared by the City Planning Commission without any consideration of the proposed Master Plan.

the most elementary arrangements of demographic, economic, and map data, as well as the more complex workings of community design, evaluations of City-wide needs (recreation, transport, education), and the intensive analyses of such special areas as the Central Business District, the waterfront, and vacant land areas. Every capital project should be developed in close relation to developmental conceptions along these lines; this requires close and continuous day-by-day attention to developmental needs and consequent capital project choices. Such competence does not exist in the present planning agency.

Capital Budget-making requires an attitude toward planning objectives to channel the development and the welfare of the City, an attitude that demonstrates concern for human needs and environmental conditions. The present negative attitude toward planning is clearly expressed in the proposed Master Plan, in which the Planning Commission states that "plans do present a nice sense of order, but one which does not have too much to do with reality. We advocate a step-by-step process that will allow us and our successors to adapt to the unforeseen."[2]

Capital Budget-making requires a construction program based on objective criteria of need rather than on political pressures. The Capital Budget should not be a tool to enlarge the planning agency's power base, as is currently the case, nor should it be a tool to put the planning agency into a central bargaining position with all other agencies of local government through its ability to withhold certain projects or lower their priority. It should be a tool to provide for public consideration capital construction programs that are objective and defensible and that are prepared with adequate perception and weighing of the City's development needs.

The Planning Commission's role in Capital Budget-making is minimal and vague. The Commissioners are totally lacking in information and orientation. Formerly, they had departmental portfolios that enabled them to gain insight into departmental needs and subsequently, share this knowledge with the

Commission-at-large. These portfolios, for all practical purposes, have been eliminated and except for
a two-day briefing a week prior to the departmental
hearings, the Commissioners are totally uninformed
on the Capital Budget. The briefings are conducted
by the acting Executive Director and a group of well-
intentioned novices who lack knowledge of budgeting
and are unfamiliar with the needs of the City. The
presentations are mere recitals of the requests of
various city departments; there is no analysis of
these requests and no understanding of their role in
policy implementation. Commissioners' questions
concerning the inclusion or exclusion of certain
projects go unanswered. It is as though the briefings
were mere formalities, necessary to keep up the
facade. The Commissioners go to the public hearings
without the benefit of the background information
necessary for informed decision-making.

Should Planning Commission Hearings
and Adoption of the Capital
Budget Be Discontinued?

The central issue here revolves around the
fulfillment of four objectives of the planning function: adequate airing of issues, objective view of
facts and values, comparison of alternatives, and
relation to overall development policy. As the present city planning agency operates primarily as a
politically oriented power, it is obvious that it
cannot function in terms of planning objectivity.
This being the case, the agency does not adequately
air the issues and does not present an objective
view of situations. It does not explore alternatives
because it has neither the desire nor the competence
to do so. It does not adequately relate to development policy because this requires information and
relational knowledge that it does not possess. Therefore, the public's reaction to such a Capital Budget
cannot be based on an assessment of the wide range
of objectives and considerations that have gone into
the preparation work. Public reaction to such a
capital construction program is based primarily on
calculations of power and pressures, for there are

no other standards by which need can be measured.

The week-long departmental hearings are merely
perfunctory. At the 1970/71 and 1971/72 departmental
hearings, the Chairman of the Planning Commission,
more often than not, made an appearance and then left
or failed to appear altogether. Even the Commissioners
do not feel obligated to attend.

The public hearings on the 1970/71 Capital Budget
were no better. At times, a quorum was not present
and the public often spoke to empty seats. After
the public hearings, the proposed Capital Budget was
immediately revised by the Planning Department staff,
so quickly that there was no time for Commission
consideration, analysis, or substantive discussion.
The Mayor's Executive Capital Budget and public
hearings were only somewhat more meaningful. After
the hearings, prior to adoption "a political package
with something for the Mayor, something for the
Borough President and something for the City Council
was fashioned in confidential negotiations on Mayor
Lindsay's Capital Budget."[3]

Recently, attempts have been made to limit the
amount of public participation in the name of "getting
projects through." On June 2, 1969, eight amendments
to the Capital Budget were approved without prior
public notice or public hearing. A public hearing
on Capital Budget amendments is not mandated by the
City Charter but is mandated by the Rules and Procedures of the Planning Commission.

In the present situation the public is the loser
when it most needs help. The difference is one of
having a Capital Budget that is almost completely
politically determined as compared to one that has
a primarily objective base plus political additions.
The difference is that of continuing planning as a
guardian of the overall public interest versus built-in
yielding to partial self-interests. The difference
is one of providing an informed basis for open public
discussion of Capital Budget issues versus the set-
tling of issues behind closed doors. The difference
is one of the ability to give plans a concrete reality

through exercising control over development powers
versus having control powers exist only on paper.
These are the realities underlying the current making
of the Capital Budget.

DEFICIT FINANCING

Deficit financing is the inclusion in the Capital
Budget of items of an annual recurring nature that
actually belong in the Expense Budget. These items
are paid for by borrowing rather than from tax rev-
enues. The amount of borrowing for these Expense
Budget items has increased from $32 million six years
ago to $158 million in 1969.* Examples of deficit
financing in the 1969/70 Capital Budget are: Human
Resources (ES 77), $30 million for job training and
related services; Housing and Development Administration, $19.1 million for such items as neighborhood
conservation offices and inspectional activity; and
Parks, Recreation and Cultural Administration, $6.2
million.

As stated previously, the City Planning Commission's role in Capital Budget-making is to base
its decisions on objective facts and values rather
than on political expediency and to bring forth to
the public forum all the issues relating to future
public improvements. Deficit financing is political
expediency, the same kind of political expediency
that Mayor Lindsay opposed in his 1965 white paper
on finances, "From Fiscal Decay to Recovery." At
that time, he stated that he would "initiate a
program that will eliminate expense budget items
from the capital budget."[4] Yet, he now describes
the use of borrowing as "contributing to bridging

---

*An analysis of the 1971/72 Capital Budget
would reveal a critical increase in such items.
According to the Citizens Budget Commission this
budget contains $150 million of Expense Budget items.
See Citizens Budget Commission, "Statement on the
1971/72 Capital Budget" (New York, December 14, 1970).

the expense budget gap."5   The City Planning Commission's approval of this type of borrowing is
fiscal irresponsibility.   It is costing the people
of the City of New York an additional $22 million
per year.   As so well stated by Mayor Lindsay in
1965, "Borrowing for the expense budget is not the
answer today, and it should never be the answer
for the financing of our City's day-to-day operations."6   It is decision-making on a purely political
basis.

Deficit financing obscures full public disclosure
of all facts relating to the budget.   The total budget
is understated, the details are obscured, and information is lacking.7   At the present time, most City
departments have Expense Budget items hidden in lump
sums in the Capital Budget.   Thus, the public cannot
react to all the measures relating to City development policy.

The Temporary Commission on City Finances considered this matter of grave importance and recommended the elimination of this practice by amendment
to the Local Finance Law.   The Temporary Commission
stated:

> The practice of bridging annual revenue
> gaps with deficit borrowing should be
> stopped.   This is important for res-
> toration of the City's high credit stand-
> ing.   Continued use of serial bonds to
> obtain operating revenues would threaten
> the City's capacity for capital fin-
> ancing. . . .
>
>   Some borrowing for current purposes
> shows up clearly.   But a large volume of
> current expense borrowing is not so obvious
> as it is included with borrowing for
> capital purposes or for various municipal
> purposes.   Thus, salaries of many depart-
> mental employees working on capital plans
> are funded with bonds issued for partic-
> ular capital projects or for various
> municipal purposes.

> That borrowing for current expenses
> is an unsound practice is generally rec-
> ognized. . . . It encroaches on borrow-
> ing power needed for other purposes. It
> is detrimental to the City's credit
> standing. It results in an unjustified
> interest cost. It conceals and postpones
> the impact of current expenses on taxes.[8]

THE CAPITAL BUDGET:
A LETTER TO SANTA CLAUS

Capital Budget-making is a process whereby
programs are determined to achieve stated goals,
through systematic analysis of alternatives and
their consequences and the scheduling of programs
over a multi-year period in order of priority. It
is presumed that once the Capital Budget is adopted
these programs are implemented. The 1961 New York
City Charter transformed the Capital Budget into
an appropriating document, assuming that the programs
would move more quickly. In fact, between 1966 and
1970 the rate of construction has critically decreased
and few of the projects have been built. According
to the Citizens Union, "A charitable comment on the
capital budget is that it is a list of good intentions.
A less charitable comment is that it is just a political promissory note which is hardly ever redeemed."[9]
The Bureau of the Budget suggests that this is because
there is a prevailing belief that the Capital Budget
is not real money.[10] In three extensive studies
conducted by the Citizens Budget Commission it was
concluded that any individual project in the Capital
Budget could "remain for long periods of time completely moribund except for sharply rising costs."[11]
The Parks Department alone has more than fifty projects "languishing," awaiting program planning
although funds were allocated as long as seven years
ago.[12]

Five reasons for the lack of construction are
clearly apparent:

1. The Capital Budget is used as a political

tool to imply commitment to projects on which it will
later renege.

2.   There is a systematic inability on the part
of the City Planning Commission and the City Planning
Department to cope with the complex policy issues
and come up with firm comprehensive decisions.

3.   The sheer magnitude of the Capital Budget
is beyond the present capability of the City to
deliver (a total amount of over $3 billion).

4.   The site selection process is inadequate
and unrelated to City policies.

5.   The Bureau of the Budget's zeal to initially
save money inevitably results in unnecessary time-
consuming delay which has an inflationary multiplier
effect and, in the final analysis, results in greater
total costs than would have been the case had the
original higher costs been accepted.

For these reasons, the Capital Budget is merely
a list of promises that sets in motion a feeling of
expectation followed by a loss of City credibility,
nothing more than a letter to Santa Claus. Years
pass with continuous reevaluation of programs while
the people wait in overcrowded courtrooms, in archaic
hospitals, and on polluted beaches. It seems as
though no one is willing to resolve the basic issues
and those projects that do get built get built by
default.13 The Bureau of the Budget states that
"Projects are thus frequently listed in the budget
and money technically appropriated long before
fundamental decisions have been made regarding, for
instance, the project's size, its relationship to
other facilities or construction programs, or even
the need for the project or the precise function it
will be serving. As a result, the Capital Budget
has become burdened with large amounts of stagnant
funds dedicated to projects which have little likeli-
hood of being built in the immediate future, or
possibly ever."14 After years of controversy, a
decision was made concerning the location and space

requirements of the Brooklyn Family and Surrogate
Courts. Then new members were appointed to the
Planning Commission and another reevaluation of the
site of these buildings began. A change in program
and an amendment to the Capital Budget (CB-70-23)
was proposed.* In the 1966/67 Capital Budget, $4.8
million was appropriated for Intermediate School
363, Brooklyn. This money was rescinded in a subsequent budget.

The lack of clearcut decisions and the inadequate
functional programming result in time delays and increased costs for those projects that do get built.
There are no criteria for design review and approval;
the scope must be determined as the project proceeds.
Projects "escalate into monuments" and they may be
built "even though they may be difficult to justify
in terms of subsequent program analysis."[15] Over
$1 billion are tied up in projects that may never
be built. In the meantime, the City's public improvement program is practically at a standstill and construction costs are rising. A study of 46 school
projects indicates that a total delay of 2,191 weeks
has cost the City $30 million (a 1.5 percent cost
increase per month).[16] The primary reason for delay
is the "total lack of anything which could be called
long-range educational planning."[17] Inadequate
planning and programming "combined with detailed
community participation in project review still
bedevil the design and construction of schools."[18]
Four sets of plans for Intermediate School 184, Bronx,
have been rejected either by the Board of Education,

---

*This amendment which was heard January 20,
1971, would have substituted the Criminal Court for
the Family Court. Again, a new proposal is contem-
plated whereby no buildings will be constructed and
the City may purchase an existing building for the
Civil Court. As a result, the City will be left
with a prime block in downtown Brooklyn which it
purchased about two years ago, and from which busi-
nesses have been dislocated.

the Local School Board, or the Bureau of the Budget.
A fifth set is being prepared. The original estimate
is meaningless.

A major contributing factor to delay is the
lack of realistic estimates of the total project
cost. Estimates are reduced to an unrealistic level
in order to politically satisfy different interest
groups by including particular projects in the Capital Budget while staying within the 10 percent debt
limit. This political factor as well as the inherent
cost-saving character of the Bureau of the Budget
result in great delay: first by attempting to design
and build within the designated estimate; second, by
having to request a Capital Budget amendment; and
finally, by having to renegotiate the original contracts, which are outdated. The City Planning Commission and the Bureau of the Budget base the original
estimates on previous cost figures that are already
outdated and no longer valid for current purposes.
The two agencies are aware that the estimate will be
higher after the architect comes in with his design
and that when the City goes to bid, the estimate
again will be higher.

In 1969, there were large numbers of Capital
Budget amendments at practically every Planning
Commission public hearing. On one day alone, June
2, 1969, eight items were amended in the 1968/69
Capital Budget (CB-68-22), an increase of $22.5
million. The reason cited was that "extra money
[was] needed to award contracts to low bidders, as
a low bid was in excess of estimated construction
cost."[19] In 1969, the cost of the New York City
Police Headquarters, after eleven years in the
Capital Budget, was amended from the 1968 estimate
of $35,262,000 to $57,300,000. On June 10, 1970,
six items in the 1969/70 Capital Budget were amended,
a total increase of $5,473,684. (CB-69-37,38,39,40,
41,42).

SITE SELECTION

Selection of sites should be based on planning

input and planning rationale, with differences resolved in the forum of informed public discussion. Prior to the 1961 New York City Charter, selection of sites for capital projects was the responsibility of the City Planning Commission, with final approval by the Board of Estimate. The members of the Planning Commission were involved in the selection process along with members of the Planning Department staff. The 1961 City Charter transferred this function to the Site Selection Board, which is composed of the Director of the Bureau of the Budget, acting as Chairman of the Site Selection Board, the Chairman of the Planning Commission, the Comptroller, the Administrator of Municipal Services, and the Borough President or Presidents in whose borough or boroughs the project is located. Public hearings are held by this Board and the approved site is submitted to the Mayor for his acceptance.[20]

Fred Rosenberg (a planner formerly with the Planning Department) points out that although this may sound like a reasonable process, its performance is poor. First, the Chairman of the Planning Commission, and not the entire Commission, sits on the Site Selection Board. The Commission itself is rarely involved. The Chairman serves at the pleasure of the Mayor and is subject to pressures from the Mayor who, in turn, has made prior commitments. The Chairman's vote may be more influenced by political than by technical factors. Thus, the independence and objectivity of the Planning Commission is compromised.

Second, disagreement between agencies, which heretofore was publicly aired at the Board of Estimate is minimized. The amount of information--pro and con--available to the public is diminished. Third, the Site Selection Board is made up entirely of members who hold their positions as a result of the political process. No independent professional view is brought forth. The Board is so politically oriented that even when the Planning Commission Chairman opposes an item, he is outvoted 4 to 1. Political considerations are important determinants but they should be only part of the final approval and based on professional input.

Fourth, the activities of the Board impinge upon the Capital Budget function. Change in location or scale of a project can seriously alter the intent. Fifth, the Chairman of the Site Selection Board is the Director of the Bureau of the Budget and gives the selection of sites a fiscal rather than a planning orientation. The history of disagreement between the City Planning Commission and the Bureau of the Budget over sites is long and detailed. The Bureau of the Budget has consistently recommended reducing the size of school sites with almost total disregard for play areas and has recommended locating facilities ignoring the population which the facilites will serve. These recommendations have been based on cost factors alone, without regard to community need, traffic patterns, or the general safety and welfare of the people.

An illustration of the difficulties inherent in the present operation of the Site Selection Board is provided by a recent decision on selection of a high school site in the four-block Ruppert Brewery Renewal Area (89th-93rd Streets, Second-Third Avenues, Manhattan). The position and shape of the particular site selected reflects a political decision to leave substandard housing on the site. The site selected makes it virtually impossible to create an adequate school and play field or a needed neighborhood park of sufficient size. An excellent opportunity for creating a new four-block residential park environment in the heart of Manhattan has been lost.

CONCLUSIONS

The Bureau of the Budget may be concerned more with cutting costs than with providing necessary programs to meet overall objectives but the City Planning Commission certainly should be concerned with comprehensive, long-range goals and objectives and with the creation of a Capital Budget to achieve these objectives. The New York City Capital Budget, a list of good intentions, indicates a lack of knowledge of the planning processes on the part of the planning agency as well as an inability to produce a meaningful

document for adequate public airing, based on an
objective view of facts and values, comparison of
alternatives, and relationship to overall development.

NOTES

1. New York City Charter, adopted November 3,
1936, effective January 1, 1938, Chap. 9.

New York City Charter, adopted November 7, 1961,
effective January 1, 1963, Chap. 9 continues the
City's Planning Commission's role in Budget-making.
Sec. 211 defines a "capital project" as "any physical
public betterment or improvement." Prior to submission
by the City Planning Commission to the Mayor of a
draft Capital Budget and Capital Improvement Plan
the Comptroller shall set forth a "Report" of all
obligations authorized to date and of "the maximum
amount and nature of debt which in his opinion the
City may soundly incur for capital projects" during
the next six fiscal years (Sec. 212). The Mayor
shall issue a "Certificate" as to "the maximum
amount of debt which in his opinion the City may
soundly incur for capital projects" (See. 215). The
City Planning Commission shall submit and publish
in the City Record a proposed Capital Budget for
public hearings (Sec. 215) based on Departmental
Estimates for Capital Projects (Sec. 213) and
Departmental Hearings (Sec. 216). After such public
hearings the City Planning Commission shall submit
to the Mayor and publish in the City Record a Draft
Capital Budget for the ensuing fiscal year and a
Capital Improvement Plan for the five years thereafter (Sec. 217). The Mayor shall then submit an
Executive Capital Budget to the Board of Estimate
and City Council for adoption.

During the fiscal year an amendment to the Capital
Budget may be proposed by an operating agency and,
after approval by the Bureau of the Budget, be submitted to the City Planning Commission. Public
hearings on amendments are held routinely by the
City Planning Commission (although not required by
the Charter). "Upon receipt of a recommendation

in writing from the city planning commission, approved
by the affirmative vote of two-thirds of the members
thereof and with the written approval of the mayor,
the board of estimate and city council may amend the
capital budget" (Sec. 224).

The power of the City to undertake the planning and
execution of a capital program for a six-year period
is pursuant to the New York State General Municipal
Law, Chap. 24 of the Consolidated Laws of New York
State, Art. 5, Sec. 99-g.

2. City Planning Commission, "Plan for New
York City, 1969, A Proposal" (New York: Planning
Department, 1969), p. 6.

3. Maurice Carroll, "Politicians Quietly Devise
City Budget," The New York Times, March 11, 1970.

4. John V. Lindsay, "From Fiscal Decay to
Recovery" (1965). (Obtainable from the Mayor's office,
New York City Hall.)

5. Citizens Budget Commission, "The Shadow
Budget," (New York, June, 1969), p. 3.

6. Lindsay, "From fiscal Decay . . . ," op.
cit.

7. Citizens Budget Commission, op. cit., pp.
4, 5.

8. The Temporary Commission on City Finances,
"Final Report," (New York: pub. August, 1966), pp.
7, 77-78.

9. Citizens Union "Statement on 1969/70
Executive Capital Budget" (New York, February 25,
1969). (Mimeographed.)

10. Bureau of the Budget, "Improving New York
City's Capital Construction Process--A Report to
the Board of Estimate" (City of New York, June, 1970),
p. 7.

11.   Citizens Budget Commission, "City Construction: Progress Zero" (New York, July, 1968), p. A-1. See also Citizens Budget Commission, "School Construction: Failures and Frustrations" (New York, September, 1968) and "City Construction: One Year Later" (New York, August, 1969).

12.   Bureau of the Budget, op. cit., p. 8.

13.   Citizens Budget Commission, "City Construction: Progress Zero," op. cit., p. A-7.

14.   Bureau of the Budget, op. cit., p. 6.

15.   Ibid

16.   Karl E. Sittler, "The Public School Planning and Decision Process," Report to the City Planning Department (New York, April 30, 1970), p. 1.

17.   Ibid., p. 2.

18.   Bureau of the Budget, op. cit., p. 10.

19.   "Report," Capital Budget Amendment, CB-68-22 (New York City Planning Commission, June 2, 1969).

20.   New York City Charter, adopted November 7, 1961, effective January 1, 1963, Chap. 9, Sec. 227.

Zoning does not operate in a vacuum. In
the end, successful zoning will depend on
the quality of the overall plan that it
implements, and on the ability and imag-
ination of the men administering it.[1]

Perhaps the most sensitive and therefore the
most susceptible area of development control is
that of zoning. A legislative device to regulate
the use and intensity of use of land, more frequently
than not zoning has proven to be an imperfect and
imprecise implementing tool. It should be emphasized
that there is nothing wrong with the concept; rather,
the difficulty lies in the practice or administration
of zoning.

Zoning is an exercise of the police power
delegated by the State to the City in the interest
of the overall community. Its intent is to lessen
congestion in the street, prevent overcrowding of
the land and undue concentration of the population,
secure adequate light and air, and promote public
health, safety, morals, and general welfare. Zoning
must be reasonable, uniform, and in accord with a
well-considered plan.[2]

The first Zoning Resolution in New York City,
approved in 1916, established regulations for the
control of height, size, area, and building use.[3]

This Zoning Resolution, though a great step forward, did not meet the emerging needs of the changing City. In the 1940's, under the aegis of Planning Commission Chairman Robert F. Wagner, the firm of Harrison, Ballard and Allen was retained to draw up a comprehensive amendment. This amendment was later updated by the firm of Walker, Vorhees, Smith and Smith under the chairmanship of James Felt.[4]

The rezoning of New York City, which began in 1959 and culminated in December, 1960, with the unanimous passage of the Zoning Amendment by the Board of Estimate, was characterized by a careful in-depth investigation of the many elements that, taken together, constitute the entire fabric of the City. It came into existence after detailed work on the part of the City Planning Department, the Planning Commission, and the consultants, as well as much interest on the part of the City's residents. A first-hand examination was made of every block in the City. Mapping and zoning changes were checked and rechecked. Over and above the formal hearings, there were more than 750 conferences and over 1,000 communications. Controversial questions were analyzed and refined in the crucible of public opinion. The resulting zoning text and maps were based upon an intensive and extensive planning evaluation of the desired spatial distribution of the City's people and activities.

Although no Master Plan existed at the time the Zoning Resolution was proposed, a comprehensive planning framework was one of the basic inputs and is implicit in the balanced and interrelated components. It is precisely this balance and interrelationship that is knowingly and inexorably being destroyed as a result of development policies that have been systematically followed since 1966. These policies have manifested themselves in a unique tendency of the Planning Commission to be realistic and pragmatic rather than idealistic. Where the previous Commissions have said categorically, "No," the present Commission has taken the position of exacting something in return. The integrity of zoning and planning has been eroded to the point

where developers and practitioners not usually noted
for their candor have publicly stated that "there
is no zoning anymore. It's all deals."5

INCENTIVE ZONING

Zoning within New York City is now called
"incentive zoning." Under this nomenclature are
subsumed the classifications of zoning by negotiation,
zoning by contract, zoning by design, zoning by
politics, and zoning by economics (fiscal zoning).
The Zoning Resolution of 1960 actually contained
the first use of this new zoning technique through
the provision for an open space bonus granted under
certain specified circumstances in carefully designated districts. With the establishment of the
Urban Design Group in the City Planning Department
and the creation of Special Districts, the use of
incentive zoning has taken hold. The idea obtaining
public amenities in return for a bonus of additional
bulk and density may seem a reasonable trade and
a rational use of the zoning tool. However, to
reach such a conclusion, it is first necessary to
determine whether the design amenities are of such a
nature as to achieve a public purpose, what the
public purposes are, what amount of bonus is commensurate with the cost of the public amenity, what
guidelines are to be publicly articulated, and
whether the benefits and bonuses are consistent with
City-wide needs.6

The zoning text changes for the new Special
Districts contain vague criteria for the granting
of a bonus. The amount of bonus is mainly at the
discretion of the Planning Commission. The amenities
and bonuses are granted without any overall study
and without any understanding of the interrelationship between land use and intensity of use to the
City's ability to provide essential services. In
the present procedure, neither the developer nor
the City knows the rules because no rules exist.
If an existing zoning section does not provide an
opportunity to use discretion in the case of a
particular building, a new zoning amendment is

approved to meet the needs and desires of the Commission and the developer.

In Lower Manhattan, practically every new building has been granted a "variance." In return, some benefit has been given to the City. The economics of this incentive zoning have not been worked out--some bonuses may have been windfalls and some amenities useless. In the case of the Uris Building, a special text change was made (CP-20131) to permit elevated, rather than street level, plazas to be counted for an open space bonus. As a result of this Special Permit and a concomitant demapping of three streets, Uris received an increase in floor area of 1.45 million square feet. In return, the City received an open plaza, three stories above street level, accessible to the public by means of an escalator.

Another amendment to the Zoning Ordinance was approved giving the Planning Commission power to grant relief from height, setback, and yard requirements in Lower Manhattan (CP-20248) where the "design of the applicant's building "is appropriate." In a letter to the Planning Commission on April 17, 1968, the Citizens Union wrote that it opposed granting this power to the Commission until the Commission developed "explicit standards for the area and formulated procedures to insure adequate notices to concerned owners." The letter stated that the integrity of zoning was in jeopardy and that without guidelines the granting of variances might become arbitrary. These variances might very well constitute "spot zoning." Citizens Union also expressed fear that this type of amendment would spread throughout Manhattan.

So numerous were the special permits granted in Lower Manhattan that the public scarcely could be informed and rarely appeared at the hearings. Notice of the permits were printed in the City Record, an official publication read by only a very few. The Commission's vote on most of these matters was not much more informed than the public's and approval was more or less pro forma. The then Executive

Director of the Planning Department was also Director
of the Lower Manhattan Office, and negotiations
were made via the Lower Manhattan Office.* The
Commission's role in zoning was lessened critically.

The fear of Citizens Union was justified.
Height, setback, and yard regulations have been
waived all over Manhattan. Permits have been granted
not on the substantive planning merits but on the
ability of the Commission to exact concessions such
as sitting areas, pedestrian walks, and street
furniture. Bargaining has become a precious tool
in the new zoning and has caused more than one member
of the Planning Commission to suggest that the
developers' belief that the Commission will make
any concession to get a better designed building
"is an invitation to extortion" or "blackmail."

In the case of the Special Theater District
designation (CP-19999,20000) and the Minskoff-Astor
Special Permit (CP-20251), the Planning Commission,
under the previous Chairman, William Ballard, denied
a request for rezoning the entire parcel to the
highest commercial bulk designation permitted
(F.A.R. 15). The developer then employed the old,
but strangely effective, ploy of showing not what
he could build but the most horrendous example of
what could be built under existing zoning. Reacting
predictably to such unaesthetic and shocking development, the Commission, under the new Chairman, granted
the zoning change. Shortly thereafter, changes in
the money market inhibited development and, con-
currently, the Urban Design Group began negotiations
for a new legitimate theater as part of the office
building complex. The developer attributed the
delay he was experiencing to these negotiations,
fixed a dollar value on the delay, and demanded an

---

*This Executive Director became Vice-President
of Uris Corporation after leaving the City Planning
Department. A briefing to the Commission on the
Lower Manhattan development did not occur until the
fall of 1970.

unconscionable increase in bulk and density as
compensation for the delay and for providing the
theater. A consultant to the Planning Commission
spoke against the need for any bonus, especially
a bonus of more than 10 percent. He was ignored.
A floor area ratio of 21.6 was granted.* The
developer himself was among those shocked by the
extent of the bonus--44 percent--and the ease with
which it was achieved. At the same time, a bonus
was granted to the Uris-Capital Corporation increasing
its floor area ratio to 20.8 (CP-20250), although
the developer already had promised to include a
theater in his development in return for a previous
map change. The increase in floor area granted to
Minskoff by the remapping and Theater District bonus
came to about 546,333 square feet of rentable floor
area or about 30,351 square feet of land at a market
value of $300 per square foot--a gain of about
$9,105,300. (The remapping resulted in 295,802 square
feet; 250,531 square feet resulted from the special
bonus.) The increase granted to Uris with the
remapping and bonus came to about 390,338 square
feet or about 21,685 square feet of land with a
market value of about $6,521,500. (The remapping
resulted in 153,588 square feet; 236,750 square
feet resulted from the bonus.)

        A Planning Department staff memorandum (September
21, 1967) recommended against the Theater District
amendment, pointing out that zoning must be rational
and that text and map changes must be able to justify
the privileges granted to individual developers.
In the absence of a plan, the City was in no position
to exact any meaningful concessions in return for
the privileges. The excessive 44 percent bonus in
this highest bulk area characterized by congestion,
overcrowding, and strained infrastructure will set
a precedent throughout the City whereby the Commission
will be unable to justify not granting such a bonus
elsewhere, where the problems are not as acute.

_____

        *Floor Ratio is the total amount of floor space
in relation to the lot area.

The Theater District bonus did not give the
Commission control over the design of all of the
buildings in the area. In the case of the Bernstein
building, efforts to locate a ballet theater within
the office complex proved futile. The developer
owned the Wurlitzer building adjoining the site but
could not demolish it because of unexpired leaseholds.
A tailor-made zoning amendment provided that a new
development on a site with an existing building with
unexpired leaseholds could borrow the total floor
area of that building and site and use that floor
area in computing the allowable floor area of the
new building. The leases would have to be terminated
in five years and a bond posted. According to the
amendment, the City would receive a public benefit
that "would result in improved circulation" and
"perhaps" a subway connection (CP-20700).

After the zoning text was tailored to fit the
site and the amendment was approved, the developer
did not avail himself of its use and instead applied
for a height and setback waiver pursuant to another
amendment. Ironically, the text change was intended
to gain control of the building because of the
important design considerations in light of the
building's location opposite Bryant Park. Yet
because of the need to construct the building to
meet the module needs of its occupant, New York
Telephone Company, few if any windows would face
Bryant Park. The openness and view to and from
Bryant Park were irrevocably lost.

Shortly thereafter, the Theater District text
was modified to meet a new situation. The Theater
District height and setback modifications applied
only to lots 40,000 square feet and over. The
Schuberts desired to build a theater on a lot of
38,000 square feet. The text was amended to permit
modifications on lots less than 40,000 square feet
if "necessary to achieve good design objectives"
(CP-20971).

Zoning by negotiation became the order of the
day. The Planning Commission had informally approved
the plans for a Tishman building only to discover

later that the staff had overlooked a coverage
violation of six floors. After prolonged negotiation,
the Chairman of the Commission told the developers
that a "canopy" would be sufficient compensation
for the violation. Almost a year later, after the
plans had been formalized, the Commission members
stated that the "canopy" was not sufficient compensation and insisted on the addition of an "arcade."
The six-story violation was never considered in
terms of the underlying planning concepts that
prohibited such a violation. The only question was
what could be bargained for in return for the
violation.

       The Special Lincoln Center District, like the
Theater District, is a classic example of the City's
incentive zoning (CP-20365A, 20388A, 21251). It
too is the Commission's reaction to an individual
situation. So anxious was the Commission to grant
a bonus in return for a better designed building
that it initiated two public hearings on the item,
each time increasing the bonus for the particular
site. (In its haste, the Commission went so far as
to schedule the second hearing in an illegal manner.)
Apparently, after the second hearing it was realized
that such a rezoning was illegal spot zoning. A
decision was made by the Chairman to create a Lincoln
Center District, granting up to a 44 percent bonus
in return for "improved circulation" and "enhancement
of the character of the area." Approval was forthcoming despite the fact that there was no plan for
the area (actually, a study of the area only had
just begun), that increased density would exacerbate
an already serious transportation situation, and
that the bonus would escalate land values and
result in the eviction of hundreds of middle- and
low-income families.*

_____

       *About a year later, pressures forced the
Commission to reverse itself (CP-21131). The inner
blocks of the Lincoln Center Area were formerly R10.
The Special District designation changed the inner
blocks to C4-7 with a bonus, enabling the realtor

An acrimonious battle concerning the Lincoln Center District flared between the City Planning Commission and the Board of Standards and Appeals over a variance that the Board was considering for that site. The cynical observers were not the only ones who felt that the real issue was not the question of whether someone would give the City away but who would do the giving. In this instance, the developer chose to take a variance because the trade-off demanded by the Urban Design Group was more than he would accept, although the original bonus was greater than what he obtained via the variance route. This resulted in the curious spectacle of the City suing itself when the Planning Commission sought to set aside, in court, the variance granted by the Board of Standards and Appeals. The Planning Commission lost the suit.

The proposed Transportation District (CP-20387) was an attempt to save Grand Central Terminal, a landmark, through the dubious use of incentive zoning without guidelines. The endangered community forcefully attacked the lack of firm guidelines, although all spoke to the need to save Grand Central Terminal. At the public hearing, Peter Blake, editor of _Fortune_, summed up the general feeling when he stated that the amendment was "drawn up in great haste and was a highly emotional response to a particular proposal that displeases some members of the Commission" and that it was "too serious a matter of planning to be determined in a moment of panic." The prestigious Economic Development Council stated that approval would "establish a precedent in which future development will be done through spot zoning by negotiation, which substitutes personal opinion and judgment for precise rules set down in law . . . Once started, a pattern will be established that will be difficult, if not impossible to reverse."[7]

---

to gain a greater return on his property. Hundreds of families were faced with eviction and the Commission rezoned the inner blocks to R8. The Chairman stated that it was unfortunate that the impact had never been considered.

This Special Transportation District, with its 80 percent scope of discretion (a 44 percent bonus or a 20 percent penalty) was not approved due to the overwhelming opposition of the real estate industry, which feared that henceforth what could be built and the land value would depend on negotiation with the City Planning Commission. Community residents were alerted to the potential dangers of the new form of zoning.

In the case of the United Nations Special District, the original plan--developed with community participation--was scrapped because of the apparent belief by the Commission Chairman (who also served on the United Nations Development Corporation) that a floor area ratio as high as 25 was desirable. The new proposal was passed by the Commission after a long and controversial period and with a split vote of 4 to 3 (CP-21014, 21015, 21017). This Special District, with its bursting of the zoning envelope and its increase in density by over 50 percent, was in direct contradiction of the 1960 Zoning Resolution which attempted to protect the low density character of the area. The area's F.A.R. 10 was never intended as a bargaining device to be whittled away. The planning approach was intended to consolidate the Central Business District without allowing it to sprawl throughout Manhattan with an adverse impact.

As the real estate industry became more familiar with the way incentive zoning was operating, a few realtors commenced further extension of the Special District system. In order to build luxury (R10) housing in other areas, the Special Lower Third Avenue Development District was devised (CP-21179, 21180). This proposal was initiated by the Commission after meetings held by the Chairman with interested realtors. Previous attempts by the Commission to rezone lower Third Avenue, changing it from a low- and middle-income area to a high-income area, had failed because of unanimous opposition from the public-at-large. A gimmick now was devised to sell zoning (from R7 to R10) for $15.30 per square foot. The money, if and when obtained, was to be put into a fund for public housing in the

area, if and when built. The rationale for the
increased zoning was that residential construction
was lagging and that an increase in the amount of
dwelling units per acre (300 percent) was necessary
to make it economically feasible to build. This
in turn would increase the tax revenue of the City.
James Felt, former Chairman of the City Planning
Commission, contended that he did not "believe
zoning is an important contributing factor to the
lack of construction" and that "housing construction
has drastically declined throughout the nation owing
to tight money, sharply rising construction costs
and impediments to the flow of federal subsidies."8

The Planning Commission's sale of zoning, the
warping of the land-use regulations to help solve
municipal finance problems, is called "fiscal zoning."
The National Commission on Urban Problems has pointed
out that "zoning favors are for sale by public
officials" and that fiscal zoning is "for opportun-
istic reasons." Rather than being based on technical
factors, such decision-making is "through the political
process."9

At the public hearing on the Special Lower
Third Avenue District, community opponents were
startled to hear spokesmen from the real estate
industry also attack the proposal. In the public
session, prestigious real estate and business groups
aired the possibility of opening up future Commissions
to corruption of zoning. In the absence of firm
guidelines, the door is ajar for private deals.
Without a Master Plan, the courts might very well
find these actions of the Commission to be arbitrary
and capricious. In addition, with the present
limited role of the Commission members, zoning by
negotiation becomes further removed from the public
process.

CONCLUSIONS

The Special Permit is a dynamic tool of planning.
Its purpose is to reserve to the City the right to
review total development plans in the interest of

the public. The granting of Special Permits without
an overall plan will provide second-best development
and will create problems for the City that may
never be resolved. The increased number of Special
Permits suggests that there may be a need for a
different approach. If a special design or a particular amenity is in the public interest and a matter
of general welfare, then zoning should be extended
to include these amenities. The Zoning Resolution
should explicitly mandate certain amenities as a
matter of right to build and, above and beyond
this level, specific bonuses should be given for
specific amenities. This would be merely an
extension of the present requirements for parking
spaces or loading berths. If subway connections to
buildings are in the public interest, why not mandate
them rather than bargain for them? If the builder
elects to include in his plans certain design amenities that may be too onerous to mandate, why not
grant a bonus as a matter of right? This would
eliminate the inequities within the present system
of negotiating and would articulate to the builders
and citizens alike their rights and obligations in
accord with a comprehensive plan for meaningful
urban growth. Such an approach also would cope with
the administrative inability of the present planning
agency to handle the great amount of special requests.
The Commission's desire to regulate the design of
buildings and its willingness to negotiate a bonus
for every proposal is creating "so great a burden
on administrative evaluation and execution, that,
in practice it is worse than ineffectual."[10]

James Felt concludes that the new incentive
zoning has resulted in a planning agency that may
no longer be "equipped for the job" and a public
filled with "suspicion and hostility." He recommends
a reexamination of the entire Zoning Resolution so

------

*The proposed Greenwich Street Development
District (January, 1971) is an example of a partial
response to suggestions previously made to the
Planning Commission by the author.

that "new zoning" will provide orderly and responsive change and "close support of the planning process."11

NOTES

1. Alan S. Oser, "Zoning Struggle Stirs Town," The New York Times (Real Estate Section), April 5, 1970, p.1.

2. Pursuant to General City Law, Chap. 21 of the Consolidated Laws of New York State, Art. 2-A, 3, 5-A and New York City Charter, adopted November 7, 1961, effective January 1, 1963, Secs. 198, 199, 200, 201.

3. See Edward M. Bassett, Zoning, (New York: Russell Sage Foundation, 1940).

4. Walker, Vorhees, Smith and Smith, "Zoning New York City" (New York: City Planning Commission, December, 1959).

5. Alan S. Oser, "Lefrak Wants to Go On Building in City," The New York Times, January 25, 1970.

6. See San Francisco Downtown Zoning Study, "Final Report" (San Francisco: Department of City Planning, December, 1966).

7. "City Planning Commission," "Proceedings of Public Hearings," July 31, 1968 and August 14, 1968, CP20387 (New York City Planning Commission Files).

8. James Felt, "Time for a Zoning Review Is at Hand," The New York Times (Real Estate Section) June 14, 1970, pp. 1,9.

9. National Commission on Urban Problems, "Problems of Zoning and Land-Use Regulations," Research Report No. 2, (Washington, D.C.: 1968).

    10. Citizens Union, "Report on Zoning and
Planning" (New York, undated).

    11. James Felt, "Time for a Zoning Review Is
at Hand," op.cit.

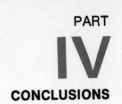

PART

IV
CONCLUSIONS

8

RECOMMENDATIONS
FOR CHANGE

If on the basis of the information in the preceding chapters it may be concluded that planning is not functioning well, it would follow that some changes should be made. A consideration of change rightfully starts with a consideration of the options available.

THE OPTIONS FOR CHANGE

In the author's opinion there are seven options for change; they are identified and discussed below.[1]

1. Continuance of a unified, semi-autonomous, independent planning commission with quasi-legislative, quasi-administrative power over zoning, mapping, and capital budgeting, and review of public and publicly-aided programs. The planning commission would develop a general long-range plan which would not necessarily be adopted by other agencies. (The New York City Planning Commission was originally created to function in this manner and so functioned from 1938 to 1966.)

2. Continuance of an independent planning commission with a small staff to review zoning, mapping, capital budgeting, and public and publicly-aided programs. Separation of the planning staff and function from the planning commission making the planning department an arm of the executive office.

(The New York City Planning Commission now informally
functions in this dual manner.)

3.   Continuance of an independent city planning
commission, but in a new role as an advocate for
local areas, developing local master plans and pres-
suring the executive and legislative branches for
implementation of these plans.

4.   Elimination of the planning commission and
subsuming of the planning function within a Housing
and Development Agency.   Planning would be concerned
with urban renewal and physical development.   The
function of zoning and mapping would be transferred
to a zoning administrator.   Final approval of zoning
and mapping changes would be by the city legislature.
Capital budgeting would be initiated by the executive
office with the assistance of the functional departments and the planning and budgeting staffs, with
approval by the legislature.   Approval of public and
publicly-aided programs would be solely by the legislature.

5.   Elimination of the planning commission and
the creation of a professional planning agency responsible to the legislature.   The functions of zoning
and mapping would be transferred to a zoning administrator.   Final approval of zoning and mapping
changes would be by the legislature.   Capital budgeting
would be initiated by the executive office with the
assistance of the functional departments and the
planning and budgeting staffs, with approval by the
legislature.   Approval of public and publicly-aided
programs would be solely by the legislature.   Formulation and adoption of the master plan would be by
the legislature.

6.   Elimination of the planning commission and
the creation of a central planning agency within the
executive office.   The planning agency would be a
professional staff aide to the chief executive,
providing long- and short-range planning services
and coordinating the plans of the functional departments.   The master plan would be prepared within the
executive office and approved by the legislature.

The functions of zoning and mapping would be transferred to a zoning administrator and final approval
of zoning and mapping changes would be by the legislature. Capital budgeting would be initiated by the
chief executive, with the assistance of the functional
departments and the planning and budgeting staffs,
and approved by the city legislature. Approval of
public and publicly-aided programs would be solely
by the city legislature.

     7. Creation of an appointed, nonpaid, advisory
planning board with power of review but with no
formal administrative or legislative functions. The
functions of zoning and mapping would be transferred
to a zoning administrator and final approval of
zoning and mapping changes would be by the legislature.
Capital budgeting would be initiated by the executive
office, with the assistance of the functional departments and the planning and budgeting staffs, and
approved by the city legislature. Approval of public
and publicly-aided programs would be solely by the
city legislature. The master plan would be prepared
within the executive office and approved by the city
legislature.

DISCUSSION OF THE OPTIONS

     Whither the independent city planning commission?
How best can the planning agency fulfill its role
in providing comprehensive long-range planning for
the future development of the City and, at the same
time, be the basis for decision-making? Where does
the planning function fit into the dynamic and complex
structure of a changing city and a changing time?

1. Continuance of an independent planning commission

     This choice will continue the separation of
planning from policy-making. The politically independent commission may continue to evaluate its
plans and proposals but its judgments concerning
these proposals may be unrelated to executive policy
determination. At first blush, a strong Mayor who
is uncommitted to planning may prefer an independent

commission, while ignoring its recommendations.
Eventually, executive programs will require statutory
approval by the planning commission and bureaucratic
delay and conflict will ensue. An independent commission, likewise, insulates itself from the legislative process.

2. A dual agency: an independent planning commission and a separate planning department functioning as an arm of the executive office

This choice will create a commission that exists
in a vacuum, has no expertise, is separated from
policy-making, and is bypassed and impotent. The
dual situation will create confusion, conflict, and
division within the planning department and between
the department and commission. The New York City
Planning Commission has evolved into such a dual
agency. The Commission's role in the area of comprehensive planning, functional planning, capital budgeting, site selection, zoning, and mapping has been
eroded. The close political relationship of the
Chairman and Planning Department with the Mayor has
effectively destroyed the Planning Commission as a
functioning entity. The planning function has been
critically damaged.

3. An independent planning commission as an advocate for local areas

Local areas will no longer accept plans that
are detailed or devised by an independent central
planning commission. Local areas will desire their
own representative planning boards to develop local
area plans. A central planning commission will find
it impossible to pressure for all the local plans
and considerable competition, conflict, and confusion
will result.

4. Elimination of the planning commission and location of planning within a Housing and Development Agency

This choice will limit planning to the very
narrow role of physical planning and development.

The economic and social implications of alternative programs, the interlinkages between systems, and the coordination of activities will be totally ignored. Comprehensive long-range planning will be impossible. Where planning and development exist within one agency, planning becomes subservient to development. Planning is ignored in favor of quick response, although the consequences of unplanned action may be disastrous.

5. Elimination of the planning commission and location of the planning function in the legislative branch

6. Elimination of the planning commission and location of the planning function in the executive office

Options 5 and 6 are similar except that the planning function is placed in different branches of government. Option 5 would be more appropriate in a Council-Manager form of government, where the Mayor may perform a primarily ceremonial function. Option 6 would be more appropriate in a strong Mayor-Council form of government. For the purpose of this study, a recommendation will be made based on the assumption of a strong Mayor-Council form of government. (For discussion of Option 6, see the following section.)

7. Elimination of the planning commission and creation of an advisory board with no formal powers

Options 4, 5, and 6 do not preclude the creation of such a board. This option may be exercised with any of these three choices.

RECOMMENDATIONS

In a dynamic and complex city, no plan "devised at one time can have permanent and flexible durability. As needs and conditions emerge and change, arrangements for meeting them must also change."[2] And so it is within cities such as New York--where

the conditions are strained beyond the breaking
point, where the infrastructure has passed the margin
of safety, where the services have deteriorated to
the edge of chaos, where the social values are in
continuous conflict, where the structure is being
torn asunder--that a new assumption, a new frame of
reference, is needed to cope with the urban problems.
Such a mechanism is planning. Locating planning
within the top layer of government will enable the
planners to deal with the broadest range of problems
and with the interactions and interrelationship
between systems and people.

The Central Planning Agency

The present-day independent Planning Commission,
no longer independent, no longer above politics, no
longer a buffer between people and government, no
longer objective or nonpartisan, no longer having
special expertise, should be eliminated. Planning
must move into the next stage--a Central Planning
Agency within the executive office of government.*
Planning will become relevant to the needs of the
City and be an integral part of the decision-making
process. In turn, the elected chief executive will
have his own planning staff which he recognizes and
accepts and on whose judgments he will rely for
policy formulation.

Twofold Role

The role of the Central Planning Agency should
be twofold. First, it should set a general framework
in terms of goals, priorities, and resources. Second,
it should serve a coordinative and interpretive role.

Such a planning agency should "furnish a unified

---

*This recommendation assumes a strong Mayor-
Council form of City government. In a Council-Manager
form, the planning agency should be responsible to
the Council.

FIGURE 2

Proposed Reorganization of City Planning Function*

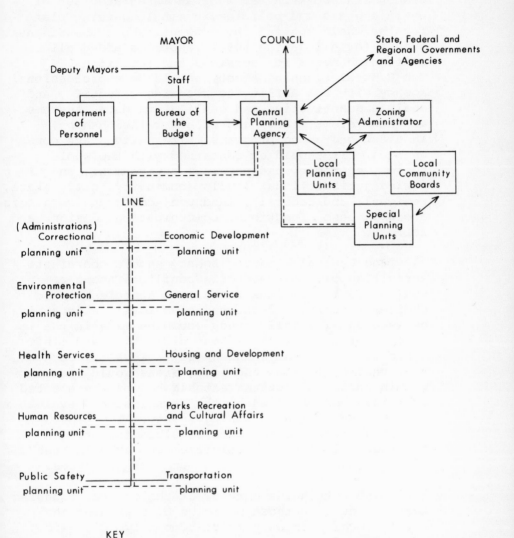

KEY

——— Responsible to the Mayor

– – – Lines of Communication, Central
Planning Agency

←——→ Lines of Communication

*This is not a complete City administration diagram.

common framework in terms of an integrated set of
overall goals and policies, a single guiding plan
for the whole spatial environment, and a comprehensive
budget for allocating total resources among all
contending needs for services and facilities."[3]
The Central Planning Agency should be a professional
agency with the ability to research, identify, and
analyze quantitative and qualitative data, systems
and subsystems, cause and effect relationships,
interactions among programs, alternatives and consequences. It should be concerned with the whole
social, economic, and physical environment, the
varied jurisdictional levels (community, city, state,
regional, and federal), land use, demographic factors,
economic base, functions, communication, design, and
ecology.

The Central Planning Agency should coordinate
activities of, and reconcile conflicts among communities and the various functional agencies. Hard
choices concerning resource and priority allocations
between equally valid needs would be made in the
public interest, with minimum disruption and minimum
waste of time, money, and energy. Ideally, each of
the functional areas and local areas would operate
within policy directives established by the elected
officials and modified by the technical and evaluatory
work of the Central Planning Agency. The Central
Planning Agency would be responsible for bringing
together all of these activities and exposing the
functional and local areas to the larger issues.

Also within the purview of the Central Planning
Agency should be those policies of a greater than
purely local interest--multi-community, City-wide,
and regional.

Eliminating the planning commission would eliminate the competition that now exists between the
Chairman of the Planning Commission and heads of
City departments. Instead, the Planning Director
and agency would become a service agency to the
functional departments, coordinating their goals,
plans, and programs within an overall long-range
framework.

Central Planning Agency Vis-à-Vis the City Council and the Bureau of the Budget

Because of the necessity and urgency of educating other agencies concerned with specific operating and major policy-making functions, it is essential that these agencies work together with the Central Planning Agency.

The City Council, the local legislative body, is the decision-making body and, as such, must be informed of the interrelationship between systems and people. There must be a reciprocity between the Council and the Central Planning Agency. The latter has the responsibility to inform the Council, to interpret and evaluate programs, and to spell out the implications of alternative courses of action. The Council, in turn, must provide guidance in terms of constraints, policy implications, and political realities.

The key to this relationship is the Comprehensive Plan. In preparing the Comprehensive Plan, the Central Planning Agency, must work closely with the City Council so that the Plan becomes a working document, a basis for future legislative decisions. The Council should also require of the Central Planning Agency an annual report on the state of the community, together with all necessary substantiating technical documentation. Such a report should spell out accomplishments of the previous year in terms of target objectives and dates, define and quantify problems, and submit recommendations for revision of the Comprehensive Plan with a view to implementing policy directives of the Mayor and Council. This should be done on a systematic and periodic basis.

Parity between the Central Planning Agency and the Bureau of the Budget must be developed because of the Bureau's immediate and direct relationship to the Mayor. This equality will force the Bureau of the Budget, with its natural inclination to saving money, to base its decisions on criteria set by the Central Planning Agency. The Bureau should be limited to alternatives posed by the Central Planning Agency

and given flexibility within these constraints.
Exceptions should be made by legislative discretion.

The Central Planning Agency should be a staff
agency similar to the Bureau of the Budget. It
should be headed by a Director who has demonstrated
administrative capability. Although he need not be
a professional planner he should have planning expertise, experience, and commitment. Heads of operating
divisions should be professional planners, qualified
and trained. Above a certain level, all staff members
should have a certain amount of planning education.
The staff, of necessity, should include persons
knowledgeable in all professional disciplines.

The Comprehensive Plan

By definition, a Comprehensive Plan is a statement of a city's goals based on an analysis of its
needs. To be more than a letter to Santa Claus, it
must be sufficiently specific to indicate, at least
in general, how its goals can be achieved. The
goals must be related to resources, but only in
general terms, since over the period of implementation
the availability of resources will fluctuate depending
upon factors completely beyond the control of the
City. These include the general level of prosperity,
degree of national involvement in such major external
adventures as the Vietnam War, possible change in
national attitudes toward urban problems and consequent increased willingness of Congress to finance
urban programs, and new national urban and rural
development policies that may stem or redirect
migrations between the nation's regions and ultimately
may even cause migrations away from existing metropolitan regions into newly forming ones.

The availability of resources is crucial only
to the programming of measures designed to implement
goals that are realizable at an early stage, since
of course, their presence will affect timing, pace,
and priorities. To tailor the Plan solely to our
present view of resources likely to become available
in the distant and indefinite future is to cheat the

people of the possibilities that a bolder and more
imaginative exercise might unearth. [4]

A Comprehensive Plan is an instrument designed
to enable a city to meet immediate as well as long-
range needs. To make good on this promise, a Comprehensive Plan must contain not only a description of
the City's problems but also a specific prescription
for their solution. Certainly, the existence of a
Comprehensive Plan must help make events develop
differently than if it had never been prepared.

The Comprehensive Plan, by its very nature,
must be broad and inclusive. It must set forth
policies and indicate the means, time, and cost of
implementing them. It is basic to planning that
both goals and the temporal periods for their achievement be made quite specific. Otherwise, overly
general statements fail to provide instruction and
guidance and implementation is meaningless. The
City needs to be told what the choices are and what
consequences flow therefrom. The City cannot be
left to the vagaries of future events. The City
must and can control the urban environment; in so
doing, the city will need to project, specify,
analyze, and extrapolate. A Comprehensive Plan
offers an alternative to muddling through by proposing
options to influence future development.

The Comprehensive Plan is based on an inter-
ventionist view of the role of government. Government
should coordinate and shape the social, economic,
and physical development of the City; government
should lead and act, not wait and react. An activist
government is in need of precise guidelines if it is
not to shoot from the hip. It needs a precise
definition of goals and a thorough evaluation of all
the consequences of specific courses of action. The
Comprehensive Plan must be specific, although obvi-
ously subject to formal modification due to new
pressures, additional resources, more detailed understanding of problems, revision of standards, and
changed attitudes.

The proposed New York City Master Plan states

that physical development is important but secondary.
The need to make such a determination at all in the
formulation of a plan is difficult to understand.
It is counterproductive to make such distinctions if
doing so precludes the kind of detailed concern with
physical development that is necessary if the City's
physical needs are to be properly identified. For
instance, even though good health care is unquestion-
ably the primary goal, can adequate health services
really be provided in obsolete substandard buildings
that are totally inadaptable to modern teaching and
patient care? Besides, physical development programs
have important economic overtones in that they are
the surest source of increased numbers of skilled
and semi-skilled jobs in the construction trades, as
well as other employment opportunities generated by
the future operation of the new facilities. Many
public physical improvements, such as schools, multi-
purpose centers, and housing, have important social
overtones as well. The goals of social and physical
planning are interrelated and mutually supportive.

In order for the Comprehensive Plan to reflect
the value, needs, and preferences of the City's peopl
it must be worked out in a synergistic relationship.
Community residents together with the professional
planner should determine the problems, sort out the
alternatives, and come up with plans and programs
that are achievable and acceptable.[5] This relationship is fundamental to the making of plans and the
implementation of plans. A plan developed in such
a manner has a large working consensus and will not
be shelved. "It will already be in the blood-stream
of the Region's decision-makers."[6]

A Comprehensive Plan is a mechanism for future
decision-making. As such, it should publicly and
clearly articulate policies and long-range goals
that are proposed, considered, finalized, and adopted
through the democratic process. As a working documen
the Comprehensive Plan should be subject to annual
review prior to the formulation of the yearly Capital
Budget and the five-year Capital Improvement Plan
and to periodic revision and amendment. The Plan
should be easily available and easily understood.

The success of the Plan lies in the understanding
that it is a document for use.[7]

The Functional Plan

Planning is not a panacea for all of man's
social ills. The failure of experts in functional
agencies to cope successfully with functional problems
in their areas of concern has led planners to usurp
the functions. The overall planner brings general
knowledge of constraints and interlinkages but he
does not necessarily understand the individual complexities of the specific functions. Comprehensive
planning has no mystique because comprehensive is
appended to it. The role of the Central Planning
Agency should be to outline the problems, objectives,
and programs. Detailing should be left to the functional agencies.

Planning units should be created within all
functional agencies. These units should consist of
professional planners with relevant expertise and
experience. Within these functional agencies, each
constituent element must have planning capabilities,
spelling out the same kind of coordinative arrangement as that on the higher level between the functional agencies and the Central Planning Agency.
The functional units should deal with quantitative
and qualitative input, past developments, current
problems, future trends, fiscal and physical resources,
long-range goals, and intermediate and short-range
objectives.

Just as it is the responsibility of each
functional agency to coordinate its internal activities effectively, it is the responsibility of the
Central Planning Agency to convene the various
agencies so that they understand their own activities
in relationship to those of other areas. Such a
close continuous relationship will insure that the
plans are implemented, that the Capital Budget and
Capital Improvement Plan reflect realistic needs
and priorities, and that the Comprehensive Plan is
not a vague political document but a realistic

optimum guideline for comprehensive City development.
The result will be the enhancement of each functional
agency's prerogatives while the various agencies
work together in a collaborative rather than a com-
petitive manner.

   In functional planning, goals must be established
For example, the New York State Office of Planning
and Coordination established a housing goal of constructing 66,000 dwelling units annually in New York
City for replacement and new households. The next
step would be to determine the allocation between
various income levels and the capability of existing
programs to meet the objectives in each category.
Then, other methods and techniques should be recommended to meet the differential between what can be
built and what must be built. There must be a determination of what kind of housing, for whom, when,
where, and how; target dates, priorities, numbers,
and resources should all be considered. Implicit
is a coordinate approach on the part of the public
and private sectors working together in a complementar
fashion.

   Public accountability may be achieved by a
mandated annual presentation by the Central Planning
Agency to the legislative body, evaluating the program
planning of functional agencies in terms of a measure
of accomplishment in reaching goals for the given
year and in terms of the long-range plan. New techniques and systems can contribute to this process
and should be utilized to the extent that they may
make a positive contribution.

                    The Capital Budget

   The Capital Budget process must be carried on
within the framework of a clearly articulated and
formally adopted Comprehensive Plan. The Capital
Budget, traditionally misused, is an instrument of
tremendous importance and sensitivity. If used as
it should be, to implement the Comprehensive Plan,
the Capital Budget will stimulate private investment
by providing a sense of public order and security.

As such, it will be a positive force in creating a
healthy community.

The Central Planning Agency must work collabo-
ratively throughout the entire year with the functional
agencies and local areas in formulating the requests
of each functional area. Review will no longer be
an activity carried out once each year in a haphazard,
uninformed, chaotic manner. Continuous involvement
will insure that the Central Planning Agency reviews
the requests comprehensively and makes necessary
modification where required to meet unmet and emergent
needs. The Central Planning Agency must develop a
Capital Budget stripped of extraneous matter that
has no chance of implementation and appears mainly
for reasons of political expediency.

In formulating the Capital Budget, there should
be a close working relationship with the Bureau of
the Budget wherein the Expense Budget implications
shall be clearly defined.

The Mayor shall submit the Capital Budget and
Capital Improvement Plan to the local legislative
body, which shall conduct public hearings and formally
adopt the Capital Budget and Capital Improvement
Plan as modified. The basis for modification shall
be publicly documented.

The preparation of the Capital Budget and the
Capital Improvement Plan will become an ongoing
process, with each year's Capital Budget having a
relationship to the previously adopted Capital Improvement Plan. The first year's Capital Improvement
Plan will be the following year's Capital Budget,
subject to modification. Such a Capital Budget will
be realistically tailored to the functional agencies'
long-range objectives and to the needs and desires
of the people. A requirement for documentation and
technical substantiation of positions will necessitate
that decisions be explained to the public, and that
the elected officials be held accountable.

Zoning

A Zoning Administrator is recommended. In New
York City, such a recommendation was made as far
back as 1960[8] but was opposed for reasons of maintaining the status quo.

A Zoning Adminstrator would provide great flexibility, expedite zoning applications and changes,
and relieve the Central Planning Agency and the
Building Department of the burdensome task of dealing
with miniscule and often unsubstantive issues.
Those issues of paramount importance such as major
land use changes, density changes, and changes having
a major impact on transportation would require review
and approval by the Central Planning Agency as well
as the local areas affected.

An open question is the extent to which the
local areas should pass on local zoning changes that
do not have a broader area implication. Another
question is whether legislative approval after public
hearing should be required on zoning changes of
major significance.

The Zoning Administrator would interpret the
zoning ordinance, conduct public hearings, notify
the affected property owners, make administrative
rulings, and pass on zoning changes after receipt
of recommendations from the local areas. A file,
open to the public, should be maintained on each
zoning change, indicating the nature of the change,
the interested party requesting the change, technical
evaluation of the change, recommendations of the
Zoning Administrator's staff and those of the local
agencies and local areas involved, and the disposition
of the matter.

Local Area Planning

In a democratic system, an important issue is
how and where those affected can influence planning
decisions. The struggle over such issues as housing

and schools are only part of the broader social
conflict between people in the communities and a
seemingly distant City government. Decentralization
or community control represents the people's desire
to participate in decision-making and to insure that
government acts responsively and responsibly giving
full consideration to the community's needs and
pressures. The cities must consider this trend as
significant and permanent and must respond by creating
a mechanism for an orderly transition to decentralization. When pressures for decentralization are
evident, an official commission should be established--
such as the British Royal Commission on Local Govern-
ment--to make a rational analysis of the processes
and problems and come up with recommendations that
precede the events rather than come after the fact.
The commission must decide how City functions and
powers can best and most effectively be decentralized
and identify the size of local districts and the
functional factors involved. The City must be
committed to a meaningful, workable decentralization
plan with clearly defined responsibilities for the
local districts and a timetable for transition.
The people must be trained in their new leadership
role and educated as to the available tools, the
use of these tools, and the interrelationships
between and operations of governmental structures.
Most important, it must be clearly stated that
decentralization does not obviate the need for centralized government and central government's role in
decision-making and action under decentralization
must be delineated.

     Local planning units should be established in
all community districts to assist the communities
to which they would be responsible in initiating
plans for local development, approving improvements
within their area of responsibility and power, and
reviewing and commenting on the plans, improvements,
and changes that are within the purview of the
centralized government. In situations involving
more than one district, coordinative, intercommunity
planning should be encouraged or special planning
units created. Certain crucial overall decisions
(such as public housing) must of necessity be made

by the Central Planning Agency, and their implementation must be mandated. The manner of implementatio
should depend on the local communities.

A close working relationship between the Central
Planning Agency and the local planning units is
essential. The Central Planning Agency should provid
the necessary technical assistance and overall guidelines. Continuous close coordination will insure
that the Comprehensive Plan reflects the communities'
needs and desires and, conversely, will teach the
local districts that their well-being depends on the
future well-being of the total city.*

CONCLUSION

Establishing a Central Planning Agency in the
executive office with auxiliary planning agencies in
functional departments and local areas will insure
the success of planning. It will spread throughout
the city planners with the same sensitivity to long-
range goals, the same sensitivity to interlinkages
between people and things, the same sensitivity to
a planning process.[9] It will insure that the adminis
trative decisions are planned choices, reflecting
the needs and values of all the people. Only in
this manner shall we create a superior environment
in which the quality of living shall be commensurate
with the dignity that is rightfully man's.

---

*The foregoing recommendations for large urban
areas do not take into consideration the borough
level of government which exists in New York City.
Cities which encompass this intermediate level of
government must make provision for planning units
within these offices so that the Borough Presidents'
decisions may be based on professional planning
factors. See Robert Abrams, "A Plan for Borough and
Neighborhood Government in New York City." (New
York: Office of the President, Borough of the Bronx,
October, 1970).

NOTES

1.   The author has drawn upon unpublished "Drafts" and "Discussions" of the New York City Planning Commission.

2.   New York State-New York City Fiscal Relations Committee, "A Report to The Governor of the State of New York and The Mayor of the City of New York" (New York, November 15, 1956), p. 65.

3.   Henry Fagin, "Planning for Future Growth," Law and Contemporary Problems 1965, vol. 30, p. 9.

4.   See Beverly Moss Spatt, "Dissenting Report," in "Plan for New York City," Vol. I (New York: City Planning Commission, 1969).

5.   See John W. Bodine, "The Indispensable One-hundreth of 1 percent," in Taming Megalopolis, vol. 2, H. W. Eldridge, ed., (New York: Anchor Books, 1967).

6.   William B. Shore, Public Participation in Regional Planning, (New York: Regional Plan Association, October, 1967).

7.   See T. J. Kent, Jr., The Urban General Plan (San Francisco: Chandler Publishing Co., 1964).

8.   See Walker, Voorhees, Smith and Smith, "Zoning New York City" (New York: City Planning Commission, December, 1959).

9.   Perry L. Norton, "Principles of Planning II" (New York University, 1970).   (Lecture.)

BEVERLY MOSS SPATT has just completed a term as a Commissioner of the New York City Planning Commission. Prior to this, she worked for the New York City Temporary Commission on City Finances which analyzed the City's role and performance in fiscal and physical planning. As a Director of the New York City League of Women Voters, she carried the portfolio of city planning.

Mrs. Spatt is a member of the faculty of the Human Relations Center of the New School for Social Research. She has lectured on city planning at many universities and has written reports and articles on the subject. Her most recent work has been her "Dissent" on the New York City Master Plan, which has been reviewed extensively, nationally and internationally.

An Associate of the American Institute of Planning, and a member of the American Society of Planning Officials, Mrs. Spatt holds an A.B. from Pembroke College of Brown University. She has an M.A. in Urban Planning from New York University's Graduate School of Public Administration where she is currently a candidate for a Ph.D.